ALSO BY ELISABETH BADINTER

Dead End Feminism

XY: On Masculine Identity

The Unopposite Sex: The End of the Gender Battle

Mother Love: Myth and Reality—Motherhood in Modern History

THE CONFLICT

THE CONFLICT

HOW MODERN MOTHERHOOD UNDERMINES the STATUS of WOMEN

ELISABETH BADINTER

Translated by Adriana Hunter

METROPOLITAN BOOKS

HENRY HOLT AND COMPANY   NEW YORK

Metropolitan Books
Henry Holt and Company, LLC
Publishers since 1866
175 Fifth Avenue
New York, New York 10010
www.henryholt.com

Metropolitan Books® and m® are registered trademarks of
Henry Holt and Company, LLC.

Library of Congress Cataloging-in-Publication Data
Badinter, Elisabeth.
[Conflit. English]
The conflict : how modern motherhood undermines the status of women / Elisabeth
Badinter; translated by Adriana Hunter.
p. cm.
"Originally published in France in 2010 under the title Le Conflit : la femme et la mère
by Éditions Flammarion, Paris."
Includes bibliographical references.
ISBN 978-0-8050-9414-5
1. Motherhood. 2. Women—Social conditions. 3. Sex role. I. Hunter, Adriana.
II. Title.
HQ759.B22313 2012
306.874'3—dc23   2011020163

First Edition 2011

Designed by Kelly S. Too

Printed in the United States of America
1 3 5 7 9 10 8 6 4 2

To Robert

CONTENTS

THE CONFLICT

THE SILENT REVOLUTION

Over the last three decades, almost without our noticing, there has been a revolution in our idea of motherhood. This revolution was silent, prompting no outcry or debate, even though its goal was momentous: to put motherhood squarely back at the heart of women's lives.

At the end of the 1970s, once women had gained access to birth control, they turned their energies to achieving essential rights, of freedom and equality with men, which they hoped to reconcile with motherhood. Being a mother was no longer the beginning and end of being a woman. Women now could choose from a range of possibilities, choices their mothers never had. They could give priority to personal ambitions, remaining single or as part of a couple, without children, or else they could satisfy their desire for motherhood whether or not they were also working.

This new freedom, however, has proved to be a source of contradiction. On the one hand, it has significantly altered the status of motherhood by implicating mothers in a raft of added responsibilities for the children they have chosen to have. On the other hand, by putting an end to age-old notions of biological destiny and necessity, it has brought the concept of personal fulfillment to the fore. Women should have a child, or two children or more, if having children enriches their emotional experience and corresponds to their choices in life. If not, they should abstain. The individualism and hedonism that are hallmarks of our culture have become the primary motivations for having children, but also sometimes the reason not to. For a majority of women it remains difficult to reconcile increasingly burdensome maternal responsibilities with personal fulfillment.

Thirty years ago, we still hoped we could square the circle by sharing the workplace and home equitably with men. We thought we were well on our way to this goal but the 1980s and 1990s marked the beginning of a profound threefold crisis that brought an end (perhaps temporarily) to our earlier ambitions: an economic crisis, coinciding with an identity crisis, prompted a crisis of equality between the sexes, halting all progress. This is evident in the wage salary gap, which has prevailed ever since.

The economic slump of the early 1990s sent a good many

women back to the home, particularly those with the least education or training who were the most economically vulnerable. In France parents were offered government assistance to stay at home for three years and look after their young children. After all, it was felt, raising a child is as much a job as any other, and often more rewarding—except that it was considered worth half the minimum wage. Massive unemployment affected women far more than it did men, and had the added effect of restoring motherhood to center stage, valued as more reliable and gratifying than a poorly paid job that might disappear overnight. In addition, an unemployed father is always considered more detrimental to the family than an unemployed mother, and at the same time, child psychologists kept coming up with new responsibilities for parents that seemed to fall to the mother alone.

The economic crisis therefore put paid to our hope that men would change. Their resistance to equality and sharing the work at home remained as strong as ever and the promising beginnings we thought we had seen went no further. Today, just like twenty years ago, women take on three-quarters of the domestic work, and since unequal division of labor in the home is the primary cause of the wage gap, inequality is thriving. But the economic crisis is not the only reason for stalled progress toward equality. Perhaps unprecedented in human history and far harder to resolve, another crisis compounded the economic damage: one of *identity*.

Until recently, the world of men and the world of women were sharply differentiated. The complementary nature of their respective roles and responsibilities fostered a sense of identity specific to each. But once men and women were able to take on the same roles and carry out the same responsibilities—in both public and private spheres—what was left of their essential differences? While motherhood remained the sole privilege of women, where is the exclusive sphere preferred for men? Are they to be defined only negatively, as people who cannot bear children?

All this has provoked profound existential disorientation for men. The question is made all the more complex by the possibility of removing men from the process of conception altogether, and by the necessity, perhaps, of essentially redefining motherhood. Is the mother the one who provides the egg, the one who carries the baby, or the one who raises the child? And what does all this mean for the essential differences between being a father and being a mother?

In the face of so much upheaval and uncertainty, we are sorely tempted to put our faith back in good old Mother Nature and denounce the ambitions of an earlier generation as deviant. This temptation has been reinforced by the emergence of a movement dressed in the guise of a modern, moral cause that worships all things natural. This ideology, which essentially advocates a return to a traditional model, has had an overwhelming influence on women's future and their choices. Just as Jean-Jacques Rousseau succeeded in doing, troops of this movement intend to persuade women to return to nature, which means reverting to fundamental values of which maternal instincts are a cornerstone. But, unlike in the eighteenth century, women now have three options: embracing motherhood, rejecting it, or negotiating some middle ground, depending on whether they privilege their personal pursuit or a maternal role. The more intense—or even exclusive—that role is, the more likely it is to conflict with other demands, and the more difficult the negotiation between the woman and the mother become.

In addition to the women who feel fulfilled by having children and the increasing number who, voluntarily or not, turn their back on it, are all those who, aware of the demanding ideologies of motherhood, attempt to reconcile their desires as women with their responsibilities as mothers. The result of these competing interests has been to shatter any notion of women forming a united front. This is another reason to reconsider how we define women's identity.

This evolution is apparent in all developed countries, but there are marked differences depending on history and culture. Women from a range of backgrounds—English, American, Scandinavian, Mediterranean, but also German and Japanese—all engage the same issues and reach their own conclusions. Interestingly, French women seem to form a group of their own. It is not that they are oblivious to the dilemma confronted by others, but their concept of motherhood derives, as we'll see, from an older notion, one that took shape more than four centuries ago.[1] It might well be thanks to this that they have the highest rate of pregnancy in Europe. Which makes one wonder whether the eternal appeal to the maternal instinct, and the behavior it presupposes, are in fact motherhood's worst enemies.

PART ONE

THE STATE OF PLAY

· 1 ·

THE AMBIVALENCE OF
MOTHERHOOD

Before the 1970s, children were the natural consequence of marriage. Most women able to give birth did so virtually as a matter of course. The imperative to reproduce was a combination of instinct, religious duty, and a sense of responsibility to the survival of the species. It went without saying that any normal woman wanted to have children, a self-evident fact so rarely contested that, even very recently, one could read in a magazine a pronouncement stating, "The desire for children is universal. The urge comes from the depths of our reptilian brain, from the reason we are here in the first place: to continue the species."[1] Yet now that a large majority of women use contraception, ambivalence toward motherhood is more evident and those vital urges sent forth from our reptilian brains seem somewhat diminished. The desire for children is in fact neither constant nor universal. Some women want them, some no longer do, others never wanted them at all. Now that we have a choice, there is a variety of options and it is really no longer possible to talk about instincts and universal longings.

THE TORMENT OF FREEDOM

Choosing to Be a Mother

Every choice entails motives and consequences. Bringing a child into the world is a long-term commitment that takes precedence over all others. It is the biggest decision most human beings will make in their lives. Common sense would suggest that people consider the decision thoroughly and ask themselves serious questions about their capacity for altruism and how much pleasure they might derive from raising a child. But does this always happen?

The French publication *Philosophie Magazine* recently published a highly instructive survey. When asked "Why have a child?" the men and women questioned responded that:[2]

A child improves daily life and makes it happier	60%
A child means continuing the family, handing down its values and history	47%
A child gives love and affection, and company in one's old age	33%
A child means giving someone the gift of life	26%
A child makes a couple's relationship more intense and stable	22%

A child helps you become an adult and take responsibility	22%
A child allows you to leave something of yourself behind when you die	20%
You can help your child achieve things you could not do yourself	15%
Having a child is a new experience, introducing something new to your life	15%
To please your partner	9%
Having a child is a religious or ethical choice	3%
Other reasons	4%
For no particular reason, by accident	6%

Total

Have children, would like to or would have liked to	91%
Do not have children and do not want to	9%

Philosophie Magazine rightly points out that although 48 percent of the answers are associated with love and 69 percent with duty, 73 percent involve pleasure. Hedonism ranks first among the motives, with no mention of self-sacrifice.

The truth is, reasoning has little role in the decision to have children, probably less than in the decision not to do so. Given the large part the subconscious plays in both choices, we have to admit that most parents do not know why they have a child—their motives are infinitely more obscure and ill-defined than those suggested in the survey. Hence the temptation to put it down to overriding instinct. In fact, the decision derives more from emotional and societal factors than from any rational assessment of advantages and disadvantages. There is frequent acknowledgment of the emotional aspect, but far less attention paid to the important pressures coming from family, friends, and society. A woman (and to a lesser extent a man) or a couple without children is always seen as an anomaly, up for interrogation. How strange not to have children like everyone else! Childless people are always expected to explain themselves, although it would never occur to anyone to ask a woman why she became a mother (and to insist on getting good reasons), even if she were the most immature and irresponsible of parents. But people who choose not to have children are spared nothing—not the sighing from their parents (whom they deny the joy of grandchildren), not the incomprehension of their friends (who want everyone to do the same thing they've done), and not the disapproval of society and the state, both of which are by definition pro-birth and have countless little ways of punishing you for not doing your duty. It therefore requires a strong will and tremendous character to make light of a set of pressures that amount to stigma.

The Hedonist Dilemma, or Maternity versus Freedom

Individualism and the quest for personal fulfillment lead future mothers to ask questions they would not have considered in the past. Now that motherhood is no longer the only source of affirmation for a woman, the desire to have children might conflict with other desires. A woman with an interesting job who hopes to build a career—although such women are a minority—cannot fail to consider such questions as whether a child would harm her professionally. How would she manage to combine a demanding job with raising a child? What effect would that undertaking have on her relationship with her partner? How would she need to reorganize her home life? Will she still be able to enjoy her advantages and, more important, how much of her freedom would she have to relinquish?[3] This final question affects many women, not only those with professional ambitions.

In a civilization that puts the self first, motherhood is a challenge, even a contradiction. Desires that are considered legitimate for a childless woman no longer are once she becomes a mother. Self-interest gives way to selflessness. "I want everything" becomes "I must do everything for my child." And the moment a woman chooses to bring a child into the world for her own satisfaction, notions of giving are replaced by debt. The gift of life is transformed into an infinite debt toward a child that neither God nor nature insists you have, and one who is bound to remind you at some point that he or she never asked to be born.

The more freedom we have to make decisions, the more duties and responsibilities we have. While children might be an undeniable source of fulfillment for some, they might turn out to be a burden for others. It depends on how much women invest in motherhood and on their capacity for altruism. Yet before they reach their decision, very few women (or couples) calculate clearly the pleasures and hard-ships, the benefits and sacrifices. Quite the opposite: the realities of motherhood are more often obscured by a halo of illusions. The future mother tends to fantasize about love and happiness and overlooks the other aspects of child rear-ing: the exhaustion, frustration, loneliness, and even depres-sion, with its attendant sense of guilt.

Recent French accounts of motherhood[4] indicate just how ill-prepared many women are for this shattering upheaval. No one warned me how hard this would be, they say. "Hav-ing a child is something anyone can do, but few future par-ents know the truth, it's the end of your life"[5]—meaning, the end of my freedom and the pleasures it afforded. A baby's first months are particularly trying: "It can't be possible to be needed this much or for me to be fulfilled by this dependence, this remorseless, inescapable anxiety."[6] And: "He nursed and nursed some more, doggedly intent on the job, chained to this programed activity as I was to the TV. . . . I woke up, I went back to sleep, it was day, it was night, no one ever warned me it would be so boring—or I'd never have believed them."[7]

For one of these writers, happiness ultimately replaces the boredom, but for the others emptiness remains the over-whelming experience and all they can think of is getting back to the outside world.

* * *

Motherhood is still the great unknown. For some, it brings incomparable happiness and enriches their identity. Others manage as best they can to reconcile contradictory demands. Yet others cannot cope and find the experience a failure yet they will never admit it. In our society, to admit that you are not cut out to be a mother, that it gives you little satisfaction, would brand you as a reckless monster. Yet this is the reality. Think how many children, at every level of society, are unloved and neglected. In the 1970s, *Chicago Sun-Times* columnist Ann Landers asked her readers whether they would still choose parenthood knowing what they knew. Of the ten thousand responses she received, an amazing 70 percent answered in the negative.[8] On balance, those people felt that the sacrifices were disproportionately large for the satisfaction they received. While the experiment was not scientific—disappointed parents were the most motivated to respond—it did give voice to an experience that is generally unrecognized.[9]

Motherhood and the virtues it presupposes are not a given, no more today than they were when being a mother was a woman's destiny. Contrary to what we might have believed, making the choice to be a parent is no guarantee of being a better one. For one thing, our belief in having chosen from a position of freedom might be illusory; for another, this assumed freedom burdens women with greater responsibilities at a time when individualism and a "passion for the self"[10] have never been stronger.

MOTHERHOOD INCREASES INEQUALITY
BETWEEN A COUPLE

We know from Emile Durkheim's work that marriage comes at a cost to women and is to the advantage of men. A century after Durkheim's investigations, subtle differences have inflected this finding, but the domestic injustice[11] persists: married life has always come at a social and cultural cost to women, not only in terms of the unequal division of household work and child rearing, but also in its detrimental effect on their career and salary prospects. Today, it is not so much marriage itself that takes its toll on women (marriage no longer being a necessity), but sharing a household and especially the birth of a child. Sharing a household, which is now widespread, has not brought an end to domestic inequality, even if surveys show that it is more favorable to women than marriage, at least in the early days of the relationship. It is the arrival of a child that dramatically increases the amount of time women spend on domestic chores,[12] while the men, in their role as fathers, invest more time in their jobs. According to François de Singly, "the scope of household chores—and the justification for them—has less to do with men's demands than with children's genuine or assumed needs. When children leave home we have quasi-experimental confirmation that the toll of conjugal life derives in large part from the toll of having children."[13]

It is true that the more qualifications women have, the

less domestic work they do and the more they invest in their professional lives—not that this means their partner does more in the home.[14] A woman's academic capital, de Singly observes, is used mainly to pay for outside help, something that less qualified working women cannot afford. The difference inspired this sociologist to comment: "The revolution in lifestyle has more closely aligned qualified women with men, while shifting them further from their less qualified sisters."[15] While professional women tend to devote themselves to their work, sometimes to the point of renouncing motherhood altogether, others make the opposite choice, particularly when work is hard to come by and poorly paid. Social inequality, compounded by gender inequalities, has a huge bearing on whether women choose to have children or not.

THE EFFECTS OF AMBIVALENCE

Since women gained control of their fertility, four phenomena have become apparent in developed countries: a decline in the per capita birthrate; a rise in the average age of first-time mothers; an increase in the number of women in the job market; and a diversification of women's lifestyles with the emergence, in many countries, of couples and single women without children.

Fewer Children, No Children

Industrial countries barely achieve population replacement (and some are nowhere near it), despite increasingly generous family policies in many of them. In Europe, the decline in childbirth is steep, as demonstrated by figures for the average number of children per family from 1970 to 2009:[16]

	1970	1980	1990	2006	2009
Austria	2.29	1.65	1.46	1.41	1.4
Denmark	1.99	1.55	1.67	1.85	1.9
France (mainland)	2.47	1.95	1.78	1.98	2.0
Germany	2.03	1.56	1.45	1.34	1.3
Greece	2.4	2.23	1.39	1.38	1.4
Ireland	3.85	3.24	2.11	1.93	2.0
Italy	2.43	1.64	1.33	1.35	1.4
Netherlands	2.57	1.60	1.62	1.71	1.8
Norway	2.5	1.72	1.93	1.90	2.0
Poland	2.26	2.26	2.05	1.27	1.4
Portugal	3.01	2.25	1.57	1.36	1.3
Spain	2.88	2.20	1.36	1.36	1.5
Sweden	1.92	1.68	2.13	1.85	1.9
Switzerland	2.1	1.55	1.58	1.44	1.5
United Kingdom	2.43	1.89	1.83	1.85	1.9

Even though there are significant differences between northern and southern Europe, the tendency to decline is universal, as it is in the United States, Canada, Australia, New Zealand, and Japan, although in some places there has been a slight rise in birthrates in recent years:

	1970	1980	1990	2006	2010
United Sates	2.43	1.85	2.08	2.10	2.1
Canada	2.28	1.64	1.68	1.54	1.6
Australia	2.86	1.89	1.90	1.81	2.0
New Zealand	3.17	2.02	2.16	2.01	2.2
Japan	2.12	1.76	1.54	1.32	1.4

While demographers do not entirely agree on the efficacy of family policies (Swedish women have benefited in this area for more than twenty years but have fewer children than American and Irish women, who do not enjoy the same advantages), these remain the primary lever in trying to reverse the trend. Every country is now asking the same questions: How to convince couples to have more children? And how to help them? Family policies tend to be more traditional, meaning that they prioritize couples, or more progressive, favoring women (apart from Scandinavian countries, few put pressure on men to improve the division of household chores), but whatever help is given to women to reconcile their family and professional lives (generous maternity leave, good child care for under-threes, flexible working hours), the majority of European women are still not disposed to reach that key figure of 2.1 children.

Interestingly, France comes close, as does Ireland, but for different reasons: the church's influence in Ireland is incontestable, while in France contraception and abortion are widely available (since 1967[17] and 1975, respectively). Immigration does not account for the higher birthrate in France; although the birthrate of immigrants is initially higher, the second generation tends to fall in line with the rest of French women.[18] The statistics are, in fact, difficult to explain. As in other countries, partnerships[19] are no more stable, and many French mothers continue to work after having a second child. Additionally, pro-birth policies are less generous or far-reaching than in Scandinavian countries.

On the other hand, few French women choose not to have children at all. This phenomenon seems barely to have touched France. One in ten will not have children (by choice or not), a proportion that has hardly changed since 1940[20] and is still "markedly lower than figures from many European countries: 17% in England, Wales and the Netherlands, 20% in Austria and 29% in West Germany, for women born in 1965."[21] In the United States and Australia, some 19.7 percent of women do not have children.[22]

Nevertheless, like most other women, the French seem in no hurry to have children, as if childbearing is no longer their highest priority. First, they work to ensure their independence by studying for ever-longer periods of time to gain access to rewarding jobs (during times of financial crisis, this process takes longer and is less reliable). Then they seek out a partner who is desirable as the father of their children. Finally, many couples decide first to enjoy their life together, unencumbered by responsibilities. The "maternal drive"[23] kicks in toward the age of thirty, and more insistently between thirty-five and forty. The biological clock pushes women to make a choice; it sometimes seems that the age constraint and a fear of renouncing all possibility of motherhood are the decisive factors, rather than an irresistible desire to have a child. The child is incorporated as an added extra in a busy life in which the women already have all their bases covered.

This is not the only or the dominant approach to motherhood—the hallmark of our times is the variety of choice. Some women long to devote themselves to a large family; some want children as well as a rewarding job; others do not want children at all; and some childless women might pursue having a child at any cost. There are undoubtedly many different ways of thinking about motherhood.[24]

Diversity in Women's Choices

To understand these factors more clearly, researchers in English-speaking countries—the first to confront the phenomenon of childless women—developed a system of classification. Catherine Hakim, a senior research fellow at the London Center for Policy Studies, identified three distinct categories: home-centered, adaptive, and work-centered, and outlined the characteristics of each group.[25]

HOME-CENTERED	ADAPTIVE	WORK-CENTERED
20% of women	60% of women	20% of women
varies 10%–30%	varies 40%–80%	varies 10%–30%
Family life and children are the main priorities throughout life	This group is the most diverse and includes women who want to combine work and family, plus the undecided and those who have not planned careers	Childless women are concentrated here. Main priority in life is employment or equivalent activities in the public arena: politics, sports, art, etc.
Prefer *not* to work	Want to work, but *not* totally committed to work career	Committed to work or equivalent activities
Qualifications obtained for intellectual dowry	Qualifications obtained with the intention of working	Large investment in qualifications/training for employment or other activities
Responsive to social and family policy	*Very responsive* to all policies	Responsive to employment policies

While some branches of the social sciences suggest that women comprise a homogenous group that strives to combine work and family life, Hakim emphasized the differing extents to which women are involved in their work. Unlike most feminist rhetoric, which argues for women's common interests, she examines the "full diversity of women's employment and life histories." This "heterogeneity of women's preferences and priorities creates conflicting interests between groups of women,"[26] which, Hakim argued, proves highly advantageous to men, whose interests, by comparison, are homogenous. In her view, this is the main reason that the equality model has failed. Compared to women, men have presented a more unified front, particularly during the "prime age" of twenty-five to fifty: "Men chase money, power, and status with greater determination and persistence" than women, Hakim wrote.[27] Even though a degree of male diversity has appeared in recent decades, it remains insignificant compared to that of women. Men who choose to invest their time in domestic chores represent a very small minority. As Hakim pointed out, in both the public and private spheres, there might always have been women ready to challenge men for power, but few men who have responded to the challenge by taking over their children's upbringing. Even in Scandinavian countries, she observed, with their generous paternity leave, fathers are not inclined to devote themselves to the family although they are guaranteed the equivalent of their full salary.[28]

In 2008 in the United States, Neil Gilbert, professor of social welfare at the University of California at Berkeley, suggested another form of classification: he distinguishes among four categories of women that correlate to how many children they have.[29] In 2002, 29 percent of American women between the ages of forty and forty-four had three or more children, 35.5 percent had two, 17.5 percent had one, and 18 percent had none. Looking at these percentages, Gilbert described four types[30] of lifestyles for women based on the importance given to work and to the family. At one end are mothers of large families (three or more children), "traditional"[31] women. They find their identity and fulfillment in bringing up their families and running their households. A high proportion of them have experience of the world of work but choose to distance themselves from it—perhaps intending to rejoin the job market later—to stay at home as full-time mothers. They believe that their children's day-to-day care and upbringing are the most important things in their lives, and they derive a profound sense of achievement from child rearing. Although they opt for a traditional division of labor in the home, this does not necessarily represent a return to the patriarchal model. Many of these women see themselves as their spouse's partner in the full sense of the term. This category of women has significantly decreased since the 1970s, Gilbert pointed out, declining from 59 percent in 1976 to 29 percent in 2002.

At the other end of the continuum are the women Gilbert called "postmodern." These are childless women, whose numbers nearly doubled in the same period, from 10 percent to 18 percent. They are highly individualistic and dedicate themselves to their careers. These women, most of whom have an abundance of academic qualifications, find their fulfillment in professional success whether in business, politics, or the professions. A survey carried out in England in 2004 found similar results to Gilbert's: out of five hundred women without children, 28 percent said they were independent, happy with their lot, adventurous, and had confidence in their ability to control the main facets of their life. "As happy alone or in the company of friends as with a partner, these women have ambitions that are not shaped by the prospects of marriage and family life."[32] Fewer than half the women interviewed agreed that having a family and a welcoming home would give them a true sense of achievement.

In the middle of Gilbert's continuum are "neo-traditional" women with two children, and "modern" women,[33] who want to earn a living but are not so committed to their careers as to renounce motherhood. These categories constitute the majority, and they are often seen as representative of all women who divide their time between work and family. But in trying to balance these different demands, "modern" women tend to tip the scales in favor of their careers whereas "neo-traditionalists" give higher priority to family life. These two groups are distinguished from the "traditional" and the "postmodern" only by a matter of degree. Mothers of two children are usually employed part-time and invest more of themselves physically and psychologically in their home lives than their jobs. (Since 1976, the number of mothers who have two children at home and are over the age of forty has increased by 75 percent. In 2002 they represented 35 percent of women in this age group.) On the other hand, a "modern" mother, one with professional commitments and one child, spends more time and energy on her work than a "neo-traditional." (The proportion of this category has climbed by 90 percent since 1976, and now constitutes 17.5 percent of its age group.)

Although these two sets of classification apply specifically to the United States, they serve to illuminate the diversity of choices regarding motherhood and lifestyles that are now available to all women.

But these choices are not set in stone. They evolve in line with the economic climate and social and family policies. Equally important are changing ideologies of motherhood and the pressures exerted on women to conform to fashionable models of a good mother. We know that the view of the ideal mother changed radically in France in the eighteenth century, from a remote, offhand approach to child raising to one that was active, exclusive, and dedicated, and this model has persisted for nearly two centuries. Feminist ideology and contraception might have subsequently opened up the parameters, but there are now opposing efforts to push women toward a more constrictive model of the good mother. The consequences, however, might end up being very different from the intention.

PART TWO

THE ASSAULT OF NATURALISM

After World War II, culture entered a twenty-year period of distinctive triumphalism. The era was marked by a rejection of social and natural determinism. Like Descartes, people hoped that humankind would prove "master and possessor of nature" as well as of its own destiny. They believed that progress in the sciences and technology would grant freedom and well-being, if not actual happiness. Women took advantage of the triumphalist mood to reexamine their status, identity, and relationships with men.

Throughout history, the march to progress has been impeded by wars and economic and ecological crises. In this case, the 1973 fuel crisis ended the glorious postwar years. The ensuing economic reversal and the backlash that followed prompted the resurgence of a forgotten ideology: naturalism, which had at its core a belief that the world is governed by natural principles.[1] Although its influence gradually extended to all spheres of the industrial world, it first appealed to women, who were immediately affected by unemployment and the disappearance of job security. The most vulnerable went back into the home; others—just like men in the workforce—felt disillusioned and resentful toward companies that could dispose of them at will, according to the whims of the market.

Among this new generation, many women also had scores to settle with their feminist mothers, and they were quick to answer the siren call of the natural. If the world of work lets one down, if it fails to offer the position one deserves, if it provides neither social status nor financial independence, then why give it priority? Financial necessity is inescapable, but some women started to think that the position of wife and mother was as good as any other, and that their crowning achievement could just as well be the care and upbringing of their children. Unlike their mothers, who were always rushed off their feet and struggled to juggle the demands of work and family, these daughters were receptive to the new order of the day: children first.

Meanwhile, there was more and more talk of the laws of nature and of biology, of maternal "essence" and "instinct," which imposed increasingly demanding responsibilities on mothers. Pediatricians and countless parenting "specialists" denounced their predecessors' wisdom—and sometimes, with a few years' hindsight, their own[2]—reverting to arguments put forward by the Plutarchs and Rousseaus who knew exactly how to make women feel guilty for turning a deaf ear to the call of nature.

An underground war is now being fought between naturalist and culturalist proponents of motherhood and, more significantly, between people who claim to act as "advocates"[3] for the defense of children (against mothers' ignorance? negligence?) and women who refuse to see their hard-won freedoms eroded. We do not know what the outcome will be.

· 2 ·

THE SACRED ALLIANCE
OF REACTIONARIES[1]

Three very different fields emerged from the 1970s and 1980s, each in critical response to a dominant cultural ethos of material and technological preeminence: ecology, behavioral sciences drawing on ethology (the scientific study of animal behavior), and a new essentialist feminism—all promising human well-being. Claiming to provide happiness and wisdom to women, mothers, families, and society, each in its different way advocated some sort of return to nature. Having tried to dominate nature and failed, we had apparently lost our bearings and were lurching headlong toward disaster. It was about time we acknowledged our error and collectively and individually took the blame. It turned out that what we thought was liberating and progressive was as illusory as it was dangerous. We had been warned: wisdom lay elsewhere, in the past.

FROM POLITICS TO ECOLOGICAL MOTHERHOOD

Political and Moral Breakdown

Ecology has been defined as a doctrine that aims to see human beings better adapted to their environment.[2] Beneath the apparent banality of these words lurks a complete reversal of values: rather than mastering and using nature to address human needs and wants, humans are instead called to submit to the laws of nature. This new doctrine rapidly sparked political debate, both in northern Europe and in the United States, where countercultural movements have flourished since the 1970s. Despite quite different societies, both continents happen to be rife with the rampant consumerism typical of triumphant capitalism. Shifting the spotlight from man's exploitation of man, the counterculture began to focus on the capitalist system's exploitation of nature, exhorting man to respect it. Some even advocated an alliance with nature in the form of a "contract."[3] This call to love and respect the natural environment came hand in hand with warnings of catastrophe and revenge: if we damaged the earth, we would pay dearly. Sooner or later, Mother Nature would severely punish her children.

As early as the 1980s, intellectuals, artists, and numerous organizations raised the alarm. We were reminded of our close connection to the many primates threatened with extinction;[4] the writer J. M. G. Le Clézio bemoaned our lost paradise, and the philosopher Félix Guattari suggested the idea of "*ecosophy*, an ethico-political synthesis for a new form of ecology that is environmental, social, and cerebral."[5] Everywhere we were urged to restore the lost harmony between man and nature. Imperceptibly, nature had gained the stature of a moral authority universally admired for its simplicity and wisdom. No longer did nature oppress man; instead, with its violation, we were courting suicide. It was therefore imperative that we stop our aberrant behavior as selfish, amoral, pleasure-seeking consumers. Industrialization, along with science and technology in its service, stood in the dock, the accused. We railed against the false well-being they supposedly brought us, and the more radical among us remembered only the pernicious effects of our abuse.

First in the firing line was chemistry, accused of every evil, given its embodiment of all things "artificial," which, by definition, is the enemy of the "natural." Apart from poisoning our food (is there anything more ruinous than the chemicals in our drinks and candies?), chemicals came under suspicion of changing our genes and working behind every scourge. We have forgotten everything we owe to chemistry—notably longer life expectancy—preferring to believe the worst of it. Of all the sciences, chemistry is the one most directly implicated in increased industrial global productivity and is therefore stripped of any shred of morality. And we all know that pharmaceutical laboratories, along with producers of pesticides and genetically modified organisms, only think of money. This might be a caricature, notwithstanding, but we do all feel some mistrust toward the use of chemicals, which leads us to rely on the precautionary principle.

The reception of the contraceptive pill since its invention illustrates our distrust of all things chemical.[6] Although millions of women have embraced this method of birth control, others, even today, dislike the use of an artificial substance that inhibits a natural process. Between 2003 and 2006, sales in France dropped from 65 to 63 million packs: "fear of weight gain, rejection of chemical products, are the main grievances" of women in their thirties. The risk of cancer, possible hormonal imbalance, and the fear of sterility are also among the reasons given. According to a recent survey,[7] 22 percent of French women think the contraceptive pill will lead to sterility.

Two writers, Éliette Abécassis and Caroline Bongrand, have taken on the role of anti-pill spokeswomen. "The difference between condoms and the pill is that the pill is harmful," they claimed. Their evidence was a 2007 report from the International Agency for Research on Cancer, which established a link between the contraceptive pill and breast, cervical, and liver cancer, and classed the estro-progestative contraceptive pill as a group 1 carcinogenic product. The conclusions of this report, which noted a slightly increased risk among *current* users (the risk disappears five to ten years after stopping use), and which were challenged by a systematic review published in 2010, inevitably fueled eco-biological prejudices.[8] We might remember that the IARC's declaration of alcohol as highly carcinogenic[9] was followed by an alarmist statement from the French National Cancer Institute recommending complete abstinence—not even a single glass of wine. In this instance, the policy of abstinence was forcefully challenged by France's High Council of Public Health, which rejected such absolutism as unfounded for low consumption of alcohol.[10]

There are also strong suspicions that chemical pollution is a threat to male fertility.[11] In 2008, in an interview between the French minister of the environment and a specialist in reproductive biology entitled "Is Man an Endangered Species?" *Madame Figaro* asked, "How do we preserve our future when the environment is hitting man in the most intimate of places?" The writer sought to dispel apocalyptic visions by quoting Alfred Spira, head of the Institute of Research into Public Health: "Men aren't suddenly all going to become sterile and the human race is not going to disappear," but that didn't help. The impression remained that man might well kill himself with chemicals over which he had no control. Thus the vilification of chemicals, linked as they are to poison and death, should come as no surprise. Any mother worthy of the name will keep them away from her children.

The Good Ecological Mother

The elevation of the ecological mother originated with the rejection of hospital procedures by women who felt these alienated them from their bodies and therefore from motherhood. Unhappy with inflexible hospital regulations, exasperated by authoritarian doctors who infantilized them, these women, beginning in the seventies, embraced birth as a natural phenomenon, not a medical procedure. Dispensing with doctors, they underwent home births with a midwife and sometimes a new participant, a doula.[12] The midwife oversees the delivery while the doula helps the future mother throughout her pregnancy, childbirth, and afterward. The doula's role, which is not medical, is essentially to give physical and psychological support. The co-presidents of the French Doulas Association explained that a doula "builds an atmosphere of trust and security with the parents, [she] helps them find information and reach decisions." During labor, "she focuses on her support role while still actively helping," offering "suggestions for comfortable positions, words of encouragement, massages during contractions."[13] After the baby is born, she offers support with "breastfeeding and day-to-day care of the newborn." What is a doula's training? Essentially, her personal experience as a mother, enhanced by an understanding of physiology, pregnancy, the birth process, the newborn, and breast-feeding. An American study loudly sang the praises of the profession: easier labor; a 50 percent drop in the rate of Caesarean births; a 25 percent reduction in the length of labor; 60 percent fewer epidurals; and 34 percent fewer instances of forceps deliveries.[14]

In the United States and Canada, where doulas have been available for at least twenty years, 5 percent of pregnant women used their services in 2002. There are no figures for the number of French women enticed by this little-known service, but we do know that between 3 and 5 percent have home births with a midwife.[15] The number is much smaller in Australia, with around only 0.3 percent of women opting for assisted home births in 2006.[16] In the Netherlands up to 30 percent of women opt for "natural" childbirth. That of course excludes epidurals and Caesarean sections, which, it has been argued, obstetricians overuse. Both procedures are accused of robbing women of the awareness of their baby's birth.

The epidural, which put an end to the extreme pain of labor and delivery,[17] came into wide use in the 1970s and quickly gained ground. Yet birthing mothers are anything but unanimous on their value. Some see the epidural as women's greatest victory, ending the foundational curse of painful childbirth; others see it is a product of a "degenerate Western civilization"[18] that flies in the face of the universal ideal that is natural childbirth; yet others feel that epidurals dispossess women of an incomparable experience.

Testimony abounds from women who wanted to feel to

the full the definitive female act of giving birth, as earlier generations did and as mothers still do in cultures considered closer to nature. One woman, speaking to *Marie Claire* magazine, expressed a commonly held view:

> Giving birth to my first baby was terrible: sixteen hours of labor, seven hours of extreme pain, and two hours of pushing for a 9.9 pound baby. Those two hours of pushing were a real nightmare, an ocean of pain where nothing else in the world mattered, where you don't even think about the baby. But then there was this incredible slithering and when my baby surged out of me, when they laid him on me, when I saw his astonished little face, it was an amazing feeling. A moment of complete happiness. Would I have felt that with half my body deadened? . . . I'm willing to go through the nightmare again just to experience that kind of birth. The hours of pain are lost in the past, but the moment of birth is so vivid that I get tears in my eyes just talking about it.
>
> With my second child, I had a Dolosal injection. . . . The labor was very cold. I nodded off between contractions, and when my baby was born, I was completely out of it. I was robbed of experiencing that birth. Women who give birth with an epidural talk about "serenity." We'll have plenty of time for serenity when we're old. . . . Do we have the right to sanitize birth, to diminish the joy by

removing the pain? Is it fair to offer women pain-free deliveries without telling them about the rewards they would have otherwise?[19]

Some women take things a step further by actively embracing the pain. We are apparently wrong to "see it only in a negative light; in some cultures it is an initiation. One of life's great rituals."[20] Pascale Pontoreau, a journalist, illustrated this point with an anecdote about the birth of her second child. While in labor she heard another woman on the ward "screaming as if her throat was being cut." She asked whether the woman had complications. "Oh no, she just has a different way of expressing her suffering," Pontoreau was told. She concluded with this comforting reflection: "For women who are used to being in control of themselves, their screams in labor are probably the first they have uttered since becoming 'grown up.' Those screams are an opportunity to release years of pent-up emotion. What if an epidural means those screams remain suppressed?"[21]

So there seems to be good suffering and bad. The first is natural, the second imposed by the medical establishment. In the 1970s, the followers of the new "birth without violence"[22] movement spoke out against the brutal, humiliating treatment of pregnant women in hospitals and against Caesareans, episiotomies, and inductions being done excessively purely to suit obstetricians. At new birthing centers, the obstetricians—Michel Odent at Pithiviers hospital, Pierre Boutin at the Les Lilas maternity unit, Pierre Bertrand at Saint-Cloud hospital—forwent traditional hospital methods to give women a different experience of labor. As French feminist and historian Yvonne Knibiehler described it:

> At Pithiviers the aim is to return to man's "ecological" primitive, archaic state; women are encouraged to give birth naked, squatting in the "wild room" after a period in a birthing pool. At Les Lilas, "plant-therapy" is used to facilitate "regression" and "break the armor" that paralyzes women's bodies. Saint-Cloud advocates "relaxation therapy." These militant ideologies are a reaction both to the rigidity of traditional medicine and to the recent rise of invasive technologies (such as monitoring) and the consequent decrease in midwives attending births. Some of these doctors denounce the arrogance of an approach based purely on scientific assumptions, comparing it to superstition. They call instead for a return to nature.[23]

Although the fashion for birthing centers fizzled out,[24] the movement for all things natural was just beginning. It is now alive and well and in complete agreement with the medical profession on a number of fronts, particularly in promoting a return to breast-feeding.

Breast-feeding on demand and for as long as the child

wants is the new goal that everyone must pursue.[25] Baby bottles are under attack—both the containers and the contents. For several decades now there has been unrelenting criticism aimed at industrially produced, artificial formula. It seems to make little difference that there is now a wide variety of formula available, that it is more and more like breast milk, or that using it in the developed world is vastly different from its limited value in countries where there are shortages of water. Bottle-feeding is still condemned with increasing ferocity. Add to this the recent discovery of a chemical substance, bisphenol A (BPA), present in bottles made of polycarbonate (90 percent), which is suspected of disrupting hormonal development, causing cancer (breast and prostate), and increasing the risks of diabetes and cardiovascular disease,[26] and of course any true mother will throw them out. Breast-feeding militants, thus vindicated, have put these findings to full use.

Finally, now that we know disposable diapers wreak havoc on the environment, yet another new task awaits the ecologically minded mother. It has been calculated that in the first thirty months of life, a baby produces more than two tons of waste in the form of diapers, and each diaper takes an estimated five hundred years to degrade. Furthermore, the millions of tons of disposable diapers used every year in France alone are responsible for the destruction of 5.6 million trees. Altogether an ecological catastrophe. The ultimate argument to convince mothers to change their ways came in the form of tests carried out by Greenpeace, which revealed that absorbent gels used in some diapers contain traces of dioxin.

So mothers are advised to use cloth diapers, which are economical and ecological and have the added advantage of encouraging early toilet-training (babies are more aware of the discomfort of being wet).[27] In France, to tackle recalcitrant mothers, the secretary of state for ecology (a young mother herself) proposed a tax on disposable diapers,[28] a suggestion that, mercifully, was not adopted. At least, not yet. But there is no knowing whether our concern with biodegradability and recycling will eventually defeat our reluctance. In London, during a recent convention of nursery products, it was revealed that an astonishing 20 percent of English babies regularly or occasionally wear cloth diapers.[29]

WHEN SCIENCE REDISCOVERS
THE MATERNAL INSTINCT

Just when we thought we were done with the old idea of the maternal instinct, it has made a comeback under the guise of science. American pediatricians in the 1970s led the way in a movement that continues to draw new followers in Europe. Its pioneers focused on ethology, reminding women that they are mammals, equipped with the same hormones for mothering as other mammals: oxytocin and prolactin.

Apart from freakish cultural exceptions, women have evolved to bond with their babies automatically and immediately, thanks to a neurobiological chemical process. If that bonding does not happen, the blame lies with the mother's environment or her own psychopathology. The studies underpinning these arguments were defended by anthropologists, child psychiatrists, and a large section of the American media, which popularized the theory. The media were far less efficient, however, in making public the scientific opposition to this conformist theory, which suited everyone so well.

Maternal instinct was back in fashion. In 1981, I argued in my book *Mother Love* that the mother's instinct is not innate. When the book's American editor wrote to Bruno Bettelheim, inviting him to contribute a preface, he responded:

> I've spent my whole life working with children whose lives have been destroyed because their mothers hated them. . . . Which demonstrates that there is no maternal instinct—of course there isn't, otherwise there wouldn't have been so many of them needing my services—and that there are many, many mothers who reject their children. . . . This [book] will only serve to free these women from their feelings of guilt, the only restraint that means some children are saved from destruction, suicide, anorexia, etc. I don't want to give my name to suppressing the last buttress that protects a lot of unhappy children from destruction.[30]

The Bonding Theory

Ten years after British psychologist John Bowlby began to develop the basis of attachment theory (emphasizing the critical importance of the bond between mother and baby), American pediatricians John Kennell and Marshall Klaus put forward a theory about the bond. They claimed the mother felt a biological need to have physical contact with her baby immediately after the birth, which was essential for establishing a proper relationship between the two. "The saga of bonding"[31] began in 1972 with the publication of an article by John Kennell, Marshall Klaus (who also promoted the doula), and others in the *New England Journal of Medicine*. Convinced that women have the same instinctive behavior as other species, they applied this notion to new mothers:

> In certain animals such as the goat, cow, and sheep, separation of the mother and infant immediately after birth for a period as short as one to four hours often results in distinctly aberrant mothering behavior such as failure of the mother to care for the young, butting her own offspring away and feeding her own and other infants indiscriminately. In contrast, if they are together for the first four days and are then separated on the fifth day for an equal period, the mother resumes protective and mothering behavior characteristic for her species when the pair is reunited.[32]

Applying their arguments to observations of new human mothers, they concluded that an additional sixteen hours of contact after the birth between a mother and her newborn enhances their bond. During this "sensitive" or "special attachment" period, a newly delivered woman is predisposed to accept her child. The contact made at this time secures the mother-child relationship and benefits the child's continued development.

The concept of a "sensitive period" for maternal attachment was very quickly institutionalized. Klaus and Kennell did the rounds of American hospitals, organized workshops with professionals, and, in 1976, published a book that had a significant impact, *Maternal-Infant Bonding*.[33] "The notion of bonding seemed to strike a chord in groups as diverse as fundamentalist religious organizations and feminists," wrote Diane E. Eyer in her critique of the theory. "Organizations promoting natural childbirth and the mass media popularized the idea. Hospitals provided special rooms for bonding."[34] In response to the despair and guilt felt by parents who had not experienced this bonding, Klaus and Kennell published another book[35] in 1982, hoping to reassure them: "Obviously, in spite of a lack of early contact . . . almost all . . . parents become bonded to their babies." In order to reassure fathers and mothers, but without losing sight of their "sensitive period" theory, they now stated: "There is strong evidence that at least thirty to sixty minutes of early contact in privacy should be provided for every parent and infant to enhance the bonding experienced."[36]

Over a period of a decade, this theory sparked a great deal of debate, not only in the United States and Canada, but also in Europe. Some deduced that the failure to bond at birth was the root cause of child abuse or of children's behavioral problems. The notion of bonding itself changed and expanded: from the connection made in the first hours after birth, it came to encompass the link joining a mother and baby during the whole first year of life.

T. Berry Brazelton, the most famous pediatrician of the time, was among those who pleaded in favor of women staying at home with their child for this period. During a 1988 television program, he explained that the first year made all the difference: "These kids that never get it . . . will become difficult in school, they'll never succeed in school; they'll make everybody angry; they'll become delinquents later and eventually they'll become terrorists."[37]

One can only imagine the panic and guilt felt by mothers forced to return to work shortly after giving birth.[38]

The bonding theory, seen as an "all-or-nothing process associated with a sensitive period,"[39] soon enough provoked an avalanche of criticism. Starting in the early 1980s, researchers in developmental psychology began to look back at Klaus and Kennell's experiments and drew very different conclusions. The eminent developmental psychologist Michael Lamb found "only weak evidence of temporary effects of early contacts and no evidence whatsoever of any lasting effects."[40] He pointed to the pediatricians' various methodological errors and concluded that skin-to-skin contact had no obvious influence on maternal behavior. Other studies demonstrated the inconsistency of bonding theory (as distinct from Bowlby's attachment theory). Unlike goats and cows, human mothers showed no evidence of reflexive behavior. Hormones are not enough to make a good mother.

Yet the adherents of naturalism—particularly those who pride themselves on their "baby-friendliness"[41] (as if all others are baby-unfriendly)—continue to advocate skin-to-skin contact in the moments immediately after birth to awaken the maternal instinct. This even became one of the conditions set by the World Health Organization for a hospital to earn a "baby-friendly" designation. In France, enthusiasts of the La Leche League remain militant about immediate skin-to-skin contact. Edwige Antier, a politician, author, and pediatrician who dispensed advice for several years on French radio, never missed an opportunity to refer to its necessity. Her many books insist that skin-to-skin contact is one of those "crucial moments" that must not be missed:

> Let us leave the mother to cradle her newborn baby in her arms. Having been prepared for birth in body and mind, she is now particularly receptive to the signals given by her child. . . . The baby sends signals to the mother, and

she alone receives them. The tragedy is that this instinctive understanding, which has been recognized since time immemorial in most cultures, is denied in our own. . . . [F]rom their arrival in the maternity unit, [mothers] are subject to practices that stifle *maternal instincts*. . . . The interaction between a mother and her newborn baby is a source of wonder, and we pediatricians in maternity units can see how important it is not to separate the child from the mother if she is to receive the subliminal signals sent to her by her baby.[42]

"Maternal instincts exist, I see them every day," Antier insists, pointing to "the latest work by biologists and specialist neuroscientists" as proof of their existence. All this is simply asserted; there are no references or citations of explanations or demonstrations. The argument is its own authority. Antier relies on the usual clichés: "From earliest childhood, a woman sees herself destined for motherhood. . . . And so little girls prepare [for it], from their earliest childhood."[43] It is surprising that this pediatrician, who looks to mother cats as her example and likes to remind us of our mammal natures, did not think to refer to Sarah Blaffer Hrdy's book, *Mother Nature: A History of Mothers, Infants, and Natural Selection* (1999), deemed masterly by American critics and published in France under the unambiguous title *Les instincts maternels*.

Primatology and Anthropology Come to the Rescue of Instincts

As a primatologist, anthropologist, and sociobiologist who sought to break away from the reactionary currents in her field, Sarah Blaffer Hrdy was not unconcerned with feminist issues, which helped account for the book's warm reception by feminist critics. She asks a good many probing questions and gives answers full of subtleties. She is not the first anthropologist to defend the importance of instincts. Thirty years earlier, Margaret Mead, whose culturalist theories are widely established, tended toward the same conclusions. "The cues parents give children and children give parents are built on innate responses. . . . The infant's gesture—frail, yet very firm—is a biologically determined way in which the new human being 'asks for' recognition. . . . The adult response contains, in addition to an innate, biological component, all that the adult man or woman has learned about the helplessness, the need and the appeal of infants."[44]

Hrdy's ideas are based on a comparison of maternal behavior in rodents and primates, including women, which is largely reflexive in the first group and inconsistent in the second. She begins with the position that maternal responses are the result of the brain's receptivity to hormones. The release of oxytocin encourages feelings of connection, in both rodents and primates, but since primates have a larger and more complex neocortex, which governs the reception of oxytocin, they display variable reactions. She notes that in many cultures, anthropologists have observed reserved maternal responses among humans during "a period of indifference" among mothers while the woman recovers from the exertion of delivery." This is confirmed by a study of British first-time mothers: "40 percent . . . reportedly felt no particular affection for their babies initially."[45] Hrdy does not see this as a challenge to the concept of instinct; she concludes that a mother's strong feelings of attachment to her baby are simply delayed for the days and weeks following birth. Even though women do not display a universal behavior pattern comparable to other mammals; even though some mothers are indifferent or even infanticidal; even though Hrdy recognizes the influence of historical, social, and economic factors, she maintains that none of these considerations invalidate the notion of maternal instinct. To her, the incontrovertible biological basis of mother love is prolactin, the breast-feeding hormone. Breast-feeding, and the closeness it fosters, is the mechanism that forges a powerful link between a mother and her child.

As a follower of Bowlby,[46] Hrdy concludes by championing a disturbingly teleological point of view of attachment.

Being attached to one's mother also initiates and then maintains lactation, with the attendant cascade of physiological consequences in the mother, suffusing her body

with a sense of well-being. . . . As pursed lips clamp tightly
onto her nipple and tug . . . just who is it that is being
caught? Within moments, the mother's cortisol levels sub-
side; oxytocin courses through her veins. As if she were
getting a massage, the mother's blood pressure drops,
oxytocin suffuses her in a beatific calm. . . . Once nursing
begins, bondage is a perfectly good description for the
ensuing chain of events. The mother is endocrinologically,
sensually and neurologically transformed. . . . As her mam-
mary glands go into production, it will be a long time
before she is again emotionally and physiologically so at
liberty to cut bait. . . . Maternity is inextricably intertwined
with sexual sensations, and it is an infant's business, through
grunts and coos, touches and smells, to make the most
of *Mother Nature's*[47] reward system, which conditions a
woman to make this infant a top priority.[48]

This hymn to the efficiency of nature leaves several
questions unanswered. If breast-feeding is the trigger for
maternal attachment, what of those who have never breast-
fed, as is the case with millions of mothers? Do they love
their children any less than mothers who did breast-feed?
And what of those women who breast-feed in the hospital
and stop as soon as they leave or a few weeks later—the
most widespread pattern in many Western countries. If,
as a biological side-effect, breast-feeding offers such great

fulfillment, why do so many mothers prefer not to continue the experience, at least until the end of their maternity leave?

In Éliette Abécassis's novel, *Un heureux événement*, the
newly delivered mother explained that to breast-feed you
have to "relearn how to be an animal." There are two types
of women, she said: "Those who don't balk at going all the
way with motherhood, and those who turn away from it,
those who accept being mammals and those who cannot
imagine it. There are those who love being animals . . . ,
and those who feel disgusted, who do it out of duty or compassion."[49] The heroine belongs to the "breast-feeders" camp.
She feels all the pleasure and happiness promised by Hrdy,
so much so that she no longer even needs to make love.

Literature and countless personal accounts reinforce this
description of motherhood, particularly in an era when
women are urged to breast-feed. Thirty years ago, Abécassis's heroine might not even have thought of nursing. Would
that have made her any less of a mother? Might she not
have been even a very good mother? There are not just two
ways of experiencing motherhood but an infinite variety, a
fact that should deter us from talking about a biologically
determined instinct. A mother's behavior is tightly bound
to her own personal and cultural history. No one can deny
the intricate relationship between nature and culture, nor the
existence of hormones, but the fact that it is impossible to
define maternal behavior specific to humans undermines

the very notion of instinct and, with it, the notion of a female "nature." The environment, social pressures, one's own psychological experience, all seem to have more weight than the feeble voice of "mother nature." We might regret or celebrate the fact, but in the end the human mother has only the most distant link to her primate cousins.

FEMINISM'S U-TURN

Within a few years, from the late 1970s to the early 1980s, feminist theory took a 180-degree turn. A new wave of feminism turned its back on the culturalist approach favored by Simone de Beauvoir, who urged that the similarities of the sexes called for policies of equality and integration (what united them was greater than what set them apart). This new wave discovered the feminine as a virtue, with maternity at its heart. Equality, the new wave claimed, would remain illusory so long as we failed to recognize this essential difference, which drives everything else. While de Beauvoir saw motherhood as incidental to women's lives and the source of their age-old oppression, the new generation of feminists claimed it as the crucial experience of womanhood, the basis on which women were equipped to build a fairer, more humane world. We were urged to return to Mother Nature, which had been too long overlooked. That return meant refocusing on the physiological differences as the source of behavioral differences, and rekindling our pride in the nurturing role on which the well-being and future of humanity depends. In its emphasis on gender difference and a female "nature," this new understanding of womanhood had a good many points in common with earlier models.

From Biologism to Maternalism

In the early 1960s, Alice Rossi, a young professor of sociology and mother of three children, set a small cat among the pigeons.[50] At a time when the ideology of good motherhood confined women to the home, she had the audacity to point out the absurdity of making child raising a full-time occupation. Then, almost fifteen years later, she published an article, "A Biosocial Perspective on Parenting,"[51] which took up the same issue, but now she defended the idea that women had gone too far in rejecting their nurturing role. Convinced by the bonding theory and adopting a sociobiological approach, she argued that biology dictates a division of work between the sexes. Maternal instincts have been essential to our survival since our hunter-gatherer days; they are written in our genes, and we remain "genetically equipped only with an ancient mammalian primate heritage," even if it had now become a set of, as she put it, "unlearned responses." For this reason, she claimed, it is infinitely preferable for the mother rather than the father to invest time in raising a child. And this greater investment by the mother should continue through the child's later stages of development, justifying the trend of returning women to the home.

Even though she was a founding member of the powerful pro-equality National Organization for Women, Alice Rossi's arguments made her one of the first to open a breach within feminism.[52] Her article, putting biology and therefore motherhood back at the heart of women's issues, came just at the right time. The battle for women's rights had ground to a halt: feminism stood accused of having failed to redress the basic problem of sexual inequality. Some feminists concluded that they had been on the wrong track, having neglected to recognize the essential gender differences or taken them into account. In the struggle to be the equals of men, women had denied their very nature, succeeding only in becoming pale imitations of their masters. Women should, instead, be proud of their separate identity and exploit it as a political and moral weapon.

A new feminism emerged, foregrounding every aspect of women's biological experience. It glorified menstruation, pregnancy, and childbirth. The vulva came to represent woman.[53] There was a powerful swing toward celebrating the sublime state of motherhood as women's true destiny, the condition for their happiness, and the source of their power. Through motherhood, it was hoped, a world damaged by men might once again flourish. On both sides of the Atlantic there was a great deal of enthusiasm for this new essentialism, celebrating as it did nature's primacy and female qualities derived from the experience of motherhood. Maternalism formed the basis for a different concept of power and women's civic role. It also had the advantage of superseding the question of instinct, which always incited heated opposition.

The Philosophy of Care, or Women's Social Code

In 1871, Charles Darwin, who is hardly suspected of feminist sympathies, said, "Woman seems to differ from man in her greater tenderness and less selfishness. Woman owing to her maternal instincts, displays these qualities towards her infants in an eminent degree; therefore it is likely that she would often extend them toward her fellow creatures."[54] A century later, the feminist philosophy of care developed a more sophisticated version of Darwin's idea, with the subtle difference that mere likelihood for the nineteenth-century scholar had become indisputable truth.

With the 1982 publication of her book *In a Different Voice*, psychologist Carol Gilligan laid the foundations for a new ethic that caused a great uproar. To Gilligan, the word *care* means a fundamental concern for the well-being of others, and the quality is considered to derive from the crucial experience of motherhood. Supposedly, women are spontaneously sensitive to the needs of children and thus have allegedly developed heightened attentiveness to dependence and vulnerability in other human beings. They therefore live by a different code than men.

Gilligan compared the feminine care ethic to the masculine ethic of justice. While justice refers to abstract universal principles that operate through impartially applied rules and rights, the ethic of care is particularist. It views the world as "comprised of relationships" and made coherent "through human connection rather than through systems of rules."[55]

Freud, it should be remembered, angered generations of feminists with his assertion that "women must be regarded as having little sense of justice" and by his further claim that they have "less capacity for sublimating their instincts than men."[56] Deliberately engaging Freud's view, Gilligan argues that women's care and concern for others is in fact another form of morality, in no way inferior to man's. To Gilligan and others, women—immersed in the experience of life and concrete relationships, and better equipped to nurture connection and to protect rather than punish—bring to the human sphere a gentleness and compassion that revitalize social morals. Motherhood—thus far seen as a private relationship—should therefore be viewed as one of two models in the public realm, as the counterweight to the abstract, rationalized society of men.

In France, Antoinette Fouque went well beyond Carol Gilligan's more subtle ideas. She claimed women's moral superiority by virtue of their ability to carry a baby: "A woman's pregnancy, gestation, is the only natural incidence of physical—and therefore psychological—acceptance of a foreign body," she declared, complementing this idea with a memorable claim:

> Gestation as generation, gesture and an internal experience, an intimate experience but also generosity, the genius of our species, accepting a foreign body, hospitality, openness, a willingness to accept this regenerative graft; gestation as integrationist, non-conflictual, unambivalent to differences, a model of anthropomorphic culture, a matrix for the universality of the human being, the very principle and origin of ethics.[57]

An approach that makes biology the source of all virtue condemns, in one sweep, all men as well as women who have not had children. The implications of such an extreme form of naturalism should prompt nothing but laughter, but in fact they are far from insignificant. And the reason this is so is because naturalism has forged a kind of consensus in our postmodern society.[58] Despite the unremitting criticism of maternalism by French feminist historians, its revival is in the process of becoming one of our society's dominant ideologies.[59]

The radical shift in the three fields involved—ecology, biological science, and feminism—concerns a tiny minority of people, principally intellectuals and militant activists. But

it is no coincidence that the ideological embrace of naturalism has occurred in all three at the same time. And although
most new mothers would probably not recognize themselves
in any of the more radical depictions of naturalist motherhood, they are nonetheless influenced by the trend. Nature
has become a decisive argument for imposing laws or dispensing advice. It is now an ethical touchstone, hard to criticize
and overwhelming all other considerations.

And like its predecessor, the new naturalism has the
ability to generate feelings of guilt that can drive changes in
attitudes. In the eighteenth century, Rousseau, along with
doctors and moral philosophers, knew just how to manipu-
late women to devote themselves entirely to their children,
to breast-feed them, care for and raise them. Children's survival depended on it, as did family and social happiness, and
even the strength of the nation. Today the arguments have
changed somewhat. In societies where infant mortality is at
its lowest, no one invokes a child's survival as the imperative for a mother's care, but rather his physical and psychological health, critical as it is to his adult well-being and to
general social harmony. Given these stakes, what mother
would not feel at least a twinge of guilt for failing to follow
the wisdom of nature?

3

MOTHERS, YOU OWE THEM EVERYTHING!

Choosing to have a child means taking responsibility for that child. Mothers with high ideals of child rearing must pay the price for those ideals. But that price has become ever higher, since we began, during the 1980s, to understand the complexities of children's development and their previously unsuspected needs. A baby is a creature with abilities and requirements that deserve respect, an individual wanting attention and interaction with the person taking care of him or her. Child psychiatrists and pediatricians have taught mothers, via the media, that they must communicate with their babies from birth, decipher their crying, their facial expressions, and their movements.[1] Mothers must be hyper-attentive, aware of how to understand and stimulate their babies. As one historian of motherhood explained:

After the lively, daring freedom of the 1970s, the 1980s brought new norms. . . . Infants are not without sense; they are able to understand everything. We must talk to them as we would to adults, explain what is about to happen to them, "give words to" what they do, consult them (if only for the sake of form) when we're going to take them for a walk or put them to bed. No more initiating potty-training: they will decide for themselves when they are ready. No thwarting their desires, lest we traumatize them or make them insecure. We must let them express themselves, do whatever they like. Even if they seem like tyrants. . . . A mother's job has become overwhelming, against a background of anxiety and worry.[2]

MOTHERHOOD AND ASCETISM

A mother's responsibilities begin at the moment the child is conceived. From that point on, she is strenuously discouraged from smoking a single cigarette (or a joint) or from drinking a drop of alcohol. Over the last several years, the warnings have grown ever more terrifying and categorical. In France, the 2004[3] Pregnancy and Tobacco conference highlighted the fact that a third of women of childbearing age continued to smoke. Nearly 15 percent of pregnant women carried on smoking into the third trimester of pregnancy, even though there were multiple risks: delayed intrauterine growth, retroplacental clots, extrauterine pregnancies. Smoking constituted one of the primary causes of premature births and the risk of asphyxia in newborns.

In light of these statistics, the National Academy of Medicine sounded the alarm and—as with alcohol—advocated zero tolerance, not a single puff.[4] Two years later, in the absence of any change in the numbers, Professor Michel Delcroix, director of Motherhood Without Smoking, an advocacy group, resumed a full-bore attack. Citing the "right of the fetus to be a non-smoker,"[5] he reminded irresponsible women that "the oxygenation deficit produced by inhaling carbon monoxide in tobacco or cannabis smoke is the primary toxic cause responsible for cellular lesions in the developing nervous system and can, in some cases, give rise to cerebral palsy and mental retardation."

American studies went further, showing that it was not enough for mothers to give up smoking while pregnant—cigarettes constitute a threat in any place where children live. Dr. Jonathan Winickoff looked at the behavior of people in relation to "thirdhand smoking."[6] Parents who believe they are protecting their children by ventilating a room in which they have smoked have it wrong, he noted. The fact that the smoke has dispersed does not mean the health risks have, too. Residues of burnt tobacco embedded in windows, carpets, and furniture are just as harmful.

The toxicity of low levels of tobacco smoke constituents has been proved. According to the National Toxicology Program, these 250 poisonous gases, chemicals, and metals include hydrogen cyanide, carbon monoxide, butane, ammonia, toluene, arsenic, lead, chromium, cadmium, and polonium-210. Eleven of these compounds are group 1 carcinogens. . . . Research has documented the association between smoking in the home and persistently high levels of tobacco toxins well beyond the period of active smoking.[7]

The alarm raised over the toxicity of smoking has succeeded in eliminating the possibility of moderation—of use and of discourse.

Alcohol suffered the same radical condemnation. The French National Institute for Prevention and Health Education (INPES) made an earnest plea to women to drink no alcohol during pregnancy,[8] from the moment of conception. INPES tells us:

Even limited and moderate consumption is not without harm and can entail significant risks for the unborn child. . . . When a pregnant woman has a drink, there is soon as much alcohol in her baby's bloodstream as in her own. . . . Alcohol can have dire effects on the fetal central nervous system. . . . Drinking alcohol every day, however little . . . has the potential to give rise to complications during the pregnancy . . . as well as psychological or behavioral problems in the [exposed] child, such as learning difficulties and problems with memory, concentration and attention span.

Beware the woman who takes even a small glass of champagne at a birthday party. "This recommendation applies to all incidences of drinking, regular, occasional, or celebratory."

What is notable in the responses to these findings is the absolutism, which is then easily applied to other spheres of motherhood. There are of course some women who have never smoked a cigarette or touched a glass of wine and who heartily approve of these injunctions. And there are others who refuse to give up their degenerate behavior.[9] But most proceed with due respect for the principle of precaution. This measured response renders the extreme injunctions all the more outlandish. In Éliette Abécassis's description, being pregnant seems not unlike taking the vows of a nun:

For me, the hardest thing was to stop drinking. All of a sudden, my partner was scrutinizing how much I drank. I couldn't take even the tiniest drop of alcohol without feeling terribly guilty. No more wild laughter, no more of the flights of freedom that come with drinking or that wonderful weightlessness after the third glass of champagne. . . . I tried replacing alcohol with something else—Canada Dry, non-alcoholic beer, carrot juice but no, nothing was the same. The basic imperative hit me with the force of a guillotine: I belonged to someone other than myself.[10]

Here, pregnancy signals the end of pleasure, freedom, and the carefree life of non-mothers. Like a postulant taking the veil, the future mother no longer belongs to herself. Her worldly life has come to an end, something only God and a baby have the power to achieve. The final image of the guillotine could not be more eloquent. We have come a long, long way from the 1970s, when pregnancy was something to be enjoyed.

THE MILK WARS

At the heart of the revolution in motherhood that we have seen unfold since the 1980s lies breast-feeding. Slowly but surely, nursing has won more and more supporters in the West. It has become a defining feature in a philosophy in which motherhood determines women's status and their role in society. By the 1970s, nursing had been largely abandoned in favor of bottle-feeding, which allowed mothers to continue working after childbirth; only a small minority of women carried on breast-feeding. The reversal of this tendency is largely due to the successful strategies and militancy of an association formed by American mothers, the La Leche League,[11] whose story is truly remarkable.[12]

It all began with a picnic in a Chicago suburb in the

summer of 1956. Two mothers, Mary White and Marian Thompson, were sitting under a tree and breast-feeding their babies. Some other women came over to express their admiration, because they themselves had found breast-feeding so difficult. To Mary and Marian, the practice was the epitome of womanliness and should be possible for all mothers. Along with five like-minded friends, they began the La Leche League (LLL) to help, "mother to mother," women who wanted to breast-feed but were discouraged by fear or difficulty. The seven founding members were Catholic and active members of the Christian Family Movement, known for its traditionalist views. They took inspiration from its model of small discussion groups offering their members mutual support.

The first meeting took place in Mary White's living room in October 1956. Every three weeks, mothers came together to talk about the advantages of breast-feeding, share advice, and help each other succeed. LLL meetings were so popular that more and more groups were set up, spreading throughout the United States: 43 groups in 1961; 1,260 in 1971; nearly 3,000 in 1976. There were 17,000 group leaders by 1981, as the breast-feeding rate in the United States rose from 38 percent in the late-1940s to 60 percent in the mid-1980s. The group leaders were given training and kept up-to-date with developments in scientific research on breast-feeding. As early as 1958, LLL published its celebrated book, *The Womanly Art of Breastfeeding*, which made the group's arguments and became the breast-feeding bible. By 1990, it had sold more than 2 million copies. The league's ambitions did not stop with the United States; the organization flourished internationally, its success due to both its admirable political shrewdness and a larger ideological shift.

An Ideological Crusade

The league's crusade relies on two clear principles. First, a good mother naturally puts her child's needs before everything else. Second, these needs are fixed by nature and we have come to understand them better over time.[13] Having adopted these principles, the LLL articulated four major themes: the moral authority of nature, the advantages of breast-feeding, the superior status of the mother, and her essential role in the moral reform of society. Although the last two, being more political and polemical, were mostly downplayed, they seem to reveal a great deal about the league's purpose.

Nature's authority is indisputable. It derives its legitimacy from its "innate, essential, eternal, non-negotiable" character.[14] As Canadian sociologist Glenda Wall has noted, since the 1980s, breast-feeding has been regarded as sacred, an act of purity, innocence, and wisdom. The league's founders see it as a symbol of simplicity in our industrial and scientific age. What could be simpler and purer than breast-feeding? The first statement of the league's principles notes, "Mothering through breast-feeding is the most natural and effective way of understanding and satisfying the needs of the baby."[15]

Breast-feeding brings mothers closer to their children and reawakes their maternal instincts, which have been stifled as much by medicine and science as by individualism and modern consumerism. With the chiding tone of Plutarch, who upbraided Roman women for not wanting to nurse their children, mothers are reminded that their breasts belong first and foremost to their babies and were created for feeding.

The league's founders developed the second theme, the advantages of breast-feeding, at length. Indeed, the list of advantages grows longer with every year and every new— and always scientific—study. The physical and psychological benefits for the baby have long been known: a mother's milk is perfectly adapted to the child's digestive system and development needs; it reinforces natural immunities and reduces the risk of allergies. The LLL pleads in favor of prolonged breast-feeding as good for the baby's health and its relationship with the mother. It is up to the child, not doctors, to decide when he or she wants to be weaned. The ideal is on-demand feeding, for as long as the child wants. And for the mother, the advantages are no less: not only does breast-feeding help her quickly recover physically from giving birth and offer natural contraception, it also protects her from breast cancer and, perhaps still more important, makes her grow "as a human being."[16]

In the last five decades an impressive number of advantages has been added to the original list. For the baby: a reduction in the prevalence and severity of many infectious illnesses (bacterial meningitis, bacterial infections, diarrhea, urinary tract infections, and septicemia in premature babies).[17] Some studies claim that breast-feeding reduces the risk of sudden infant death syndrome, type 1 and 2 diabetes, lymphoma, leukemia, childhood Hodgkin's disease, obesity, hypercholesterolemia, asthma, even multiple sclerosis. Others have tried to demonstrate that breast-fed children show better cognitive development. The benefits to the mother have grown as well: a better relationship with the child, as well as prevention of postnatal depression, hemorrhages, infections, anemia, and—most notably—ovarian cancer and osteoporosis. And, the cherry on the cake: breast-feeding speeds the mother's return to her pre-pregnancy weight.

Some of these advantages—enhanced immunity, for example—are proven, on condition that breast-feeding continues for three to six months. Others are not. To date, the Society of French Pediatrics has published the most objective report on the subject,[18] pointing out areas of uncertainty and bias. The assertion that mother's milk is superior for the child's intellectual development has proved unfounded. Researchers, it seems, failed to adequately account for the mother's social, economic, family, and cultural circumstances.[19]

In the last fifteen years or so, two new kinds of arguments have appeared in pro-breast-feeding literature, one economic, the other ecological. In 1994, pediatrician Pierre Bitoun calculated the cost of "artificial" feeding at 4,640 French francs per child in the first year, approximately $800 at the time.[20] To reach this result, the author calculated the cost of formula for the first twelve months, along with the cost of equipment (bottles, sterilizer, etc.), water, and electricity. Add to that the medical savings associated with illnesses that are "avoidable" through breast-feeding, as well as the cost of contraception for the first six months, and we come to the overall figure of approximately $2,000.[21] The second argument points to the ecological benefits of breast-feeding, which saves on fuel and resources: water for the formula and washing the bottles; energy to heat the formula; the metal, plastic, and paper for the cans of formula; the energy required to transform cow's milk into formula.[22]

The conclusion is irrefutable: a good mother breast-feeds. To make this crystal clear, the league articulated the ten fundamental points of its philosophy.[23]

1. Mothering through breastfeeding is the most natural and effective way of understanding and satisfying the needs of the baby.
2. Mother and baby need to be together early and often to establish a satisfying relationship and an adequate milk supply.
3. In the early years, the baby has an intense need to be with his mother which is as basic as his need for food.
4. Breast milk is the superior infant food.
5. For the healthy, full-term baby, breast milk is the only

food necessary until baby shows signs of needing solids, about the middle of the first year after birth.

6. Ideally the breastfeeding relationship will continue until the baby outgrows the need.

7. Alert and active participation by the mother in childbirth is a help in getting breastfeeding off to a good start.

8. Breastfeeding is enhanced and the nursing couple sustained by the loving support, help and companionship of the baby's father.

9. Good nutrition means eating a well-balanced and varied diet of foods in as close to their natural state as possible.

10. From infancy on, children need loving guidance which reflects acceptance of their capabilities and sensitivity to their feelings.

Today, these ten statements have evolved into The Ten Commandments of Breastfeeding, which appear on the Alternamoms website and are biblical in form and tone.[24] Rules and advice have been supplanted by sacred law, each one requiring commentary:

I AM THE MILK OF YOUR BREASTS, YOU SHALL HAVE NO OTHER FORM OF INFANT NUTRITION IN YOUR HOUSE. Free formula samples are very tempting, especially when that two week growth spurt hits. But they have a price tag—for every bottle of formula your child drinks, your milk supply will dwindle. When the case of formula arrives, ship it off to the nearest food pantry. Don't let it remain in your house.

YOU WILL HAVE NO ARTIFICIAL VERSIONS OF MY SHAPE, NOT IN LATEX OR SILICONE, NOT ATTACHED TO A PLASTIC DISC OR A BOTTLE. No pacifiers, no bottles of water, and no bottles of formula. If baby wants to suck, offer your breast. S/he is quite possibly going through a growth spurt and is trying to increase your supply.

YOU WILL CONTACT LA LECHE LEAGUE IN YOUR THIRD TRIMESTER AND ATTEND MEETINGS, ESPE-CIALLY IF YOU HAVE NEVER SEEN OTHER WOMEN NURSE THEIR CHILDREN. Watch other women who are nursing their children with great interest, and ask questions, even if they sound silly and dumb. Most moms today were not lucky to see their mothers nurse—if you haven't seen women actually breastfeed, make sure you go to an LLL meeting. Nursing is an art, and you can't always pick it up by just read-ing a book.

YOU WILL SURROUND YOURSELF WITH PROFESSION-ALS WHO ARE KNOWLEDGEABLE ABOUT HUMAN LAC-TATION, FROM THE MOMENT YOU GIVE BIRTH. If you are giving birth in a hospital, see what their policies about artificial nipples/pacifiers are before you go. There are still nurses out there who think nipple confusion is a myth. The best cure for this is rooming-in. Or not going to the hospital at all. Also, make sure your child's doctor is well-informed about breastfeeding.

YOU SHALL NOT GIVE UP. Not in two days, not in two weeks, not in two months. If your nipples are sore, find some help before they start bleeding and cracking. If you don't think the baby is getting enough, count wet and soiled diapers. If your baby is nursing and nursing and nursing with no end in sight, find something good on the television and let that baby nurse! Feeding a baby formula is NOT easier!

YOU SHALL NOT LISTEN TO THOSE WHO SAY YOU CANNOT BREASTFEED, OR THAT YOU ARE BREAST-FEEDING TOO LONG, OR TOO OFTEN, OR TOO MUCH. Ignore your well-meaning but ignorant mother-in-law who tells you that the baby would be sleeping through the night by now if s/he was on formula. Don't pay attention to your mother who says that if you breastfeed no one else will be able to feed the baby, so you should feed formula. . . .

YOU SHALL NOT WEAN YOUR CHILDREN FOR THE SAKE OF CONVENIENCE. Research has shown that children are biologically meant to be weaned somewhere between the ages of $3\frac{1}{2}$ and 7.

YOU SHALL NOT ALLOW OTHERS TO PASS ON MISIN-FORMATION ABOUT BREASTFEEDING, HUMAN LACTA-TION, THE NEEDS OF BABIES AND EXTENDED NURSING. This includes doctors, books at the bookstore, your relatives, people on the Internet, and anyone else who doesn't have the facts straight.

YOU SHALL NOT REMAIN SILENT. Support nursing mothers whenever and wherever you see them, even if it is only with a kind word and a knowing smile. If you see an expecting mother, strike up a casual conversation. Make sure she knows the facts, or at least that there's a LLL group in your area. If you're nursing your child in public and someone comments, use that as an opportunity to educate that person. Other children are fascinated by nursing babies—and are at the best age to make a lasting positive impression. If you can't help with this generation, you can help with the next.

The league's supporters have clearly declared war on bottles and formula, and implicitly on mothers returning to work.[25] A mother who breast-feeds on demand is a full-time mother, which is why the LLL has always encouraged its followers to stay at home.

In the 1981 edition of *The Womanly Art of Breastfeeding*, the only justification for mothers working is financial necessity. Group leaders not encourage mothers to return to work. Most of them do not work outside the home.[26] The obvious result is that breast-feeding rates are higher among professional, well-paid women than blue-collar and office workers.

To maintain the strength of its influence, the LLL eventually softened its position, adding a chapter to the book in 1987 that aimed to help women breast-feed even after their return to work. It recommends using a breast pump, which enables the mother to collect the precious milk and refrigerate it to be consumed in her absence. But this is only a limited solution to the difficulties facing working mothers, not least because many women find pumping repulsive. More important, it does not resolve the essential problem of child care.

Finding someone capable and trustworthy with whom to leave a child is both difficult and expensive. Mothers are strenuously advised not to use day-care centers for babies under one year. Edwige Antier, a faithful LLL activist, never misses an opportunity to discourage mothers from resorting to day care. "When it's time for her to entrust her baby to this noisy and fairly anonymous world . . . the mother cries."[27] "As soon as the baby goes to day care, he catches all the other children's viruses, colds, bronchiolitis, etc. If he falls ill frequently and is often prescribed antibiotics, an alternative to community child care must be found."[28] And finally, this startling question: "Aren't we killing our babies by taking them away from their mothers too soon?"[29]

Clearly, under these circumstances, the best solution for both mother and baby is for women to stay at home. To convince them to do so, the value of motherhood needs to be elevated, which has been done successfully in the past.[30] This ties into the LLL's fourth theme, moral reform: mothers who breast-feed and stay at home have a significant social role to play. The well-adjusted development of their children will benefit all society. Breast-feeding is the perfect foundation for a good relationship between parent and child; it thus reinforces family ties and promotes social cohesion. The mission of breast-feeding mothers is nothing less than far-reaching civic reform: "Every mother who breastfeeds her baby is a key player in social change,"[31] promises the league. Could any duty be more urgent?

Inevitably, women who do not heed the call feel guilty. Mothers who choose to bottle-feed will not form the same physical attachment to their babies as mothers who nurse. Gregory White, husband of one of the league's founders, a doctor, said that a woman who bottle-fed was "handicapped. She may turn out to be a pretty good mother, but she could have been a lot better mother if she had breast-fed."[32] More recently, the league has called for the shaming of women who do not breast-feed, as with mothers who smoke or drink: "Doctors have no hesitation whatsoever about making parents feel guilty about not using a car seat . . . by contrast, breastfeeding is often treated as a choice."[33] But it is not—it is a duty to protect the baby from the "harm caused by artificial baby milk."

As far as the LLL is concerned, all mothers should be able to breast-feed. There are no naturally insurmountable difficulties, physical or psychological. There is no such thing as maternal ambivalence and women who balk at submitting are simply reckless or bad. Although the LLL has toned down its mission in certain countries, like France, to make it more palatable, the credo has nonetheless gained ground over the last twenty years, thanks to some unexpected supporters.

A Far-Reaching Political Strategy

Since its creation, the La Leche League has been adept at forming alliances with other movements that do not necessarily share all its claims. It has even succeeded in passing itself off as a progressive force. These alliances have extended the league's influence far beyond the traditional suburban women who were its original followers and has allowed it to give the impression that its message is universal and applies to all women.

In the 1960s, the league joined forces with the counterculture movement advocating a return to nature. According to historian Lynn Y. Weiner, "League founders believed that the 'hippie movement' aided in the popularization of the league . . . because their rebellion against the establishment included the medical establishment."[34] But tensions emerged in the 1970s when militants asked the league to take a stand on sensitive questions like family planning, ecological politics, and abortion. The league stubbornly refused, arguing that its message of good motherhood through breast-feeding should not be diluted with other causes, which would cause it to lose followers.

A more profitable alliance was formed with those parts of the medical community that supported new birthing techniques and the theory of bonding and rejected the medicalization of motherhood. In 1968, the *Journal of Paediatrics* published "A Salute to the Leche League International," wishing it well. In 1974, the American Medical Association accredited the league to provide continuing medical education, and T. Berry Brazelton, the baby guru, was one of its closest allies. In 1997, it received the supreme sanction: the American Academy of Pediatrics recommended breast-feeding for at least the first twelve months of a baby's life. The league had won the support of the full American medical fraternity.

Finally, by presenting themselves from the outset as feminists, militantly fighting for women's right to control their bodies, the LLL made common cause with the new movement of maternalist feminists. Both groups opposed intrusive medical intervention in maternity wards, and both advocated natural childbirth and breast-feeding. Even though there were disagreements, particularly over abortion and working mothers, the two groups shared a core vision of women as being "by nature" more in tune with the needs of others, more social and peaceable than men. In their view, maternalism was a liberating form of humanism. On basic questions, then, the league identified closely with the feminist ethics of care.

In addition to its policy of forming alliances, the league managed to adapt its views without losing sight of its first principles. By advising the use of breast pumps, it maintained a connection to the increasing number of women working outside the home. Through flexibility and compromise, an organization that looked like a sect in its early days succeeded in turning itself into a powerful network of national significance.

An ideology convinced of its contribution to the good of mankind does not stop at its own borders. The league set up branches in Quebec in 1960, France in 1973, and Switzerland in 1981. Today it has a presence in almost sixty countries. Princess Grace of Monaco was one of the first public figures to support the league and promote it across Europe in the early 1970s. Having identified the causes of decline in breast-feeding (lack of information and support for mothers; opposition by hospitals and health professionals; and aggressive marketing of milk substitutes, bottles, and pacifiers), league branches in different countries formed a common plan of attack.

The first enemy to tackle was the formula industry, which had expanded its won market share throughout the 1960s and 1970s. The league scored a decisive victory when the disastrous effects of using formula in poor countries were exposed. Unsafe water, poor hygiene, and high temperatures turned formula into a killer potion.[35] When the World Health Organization and UNICEF investigated the problem, the league gained unexpected support. As early as October 1979, the league sent representatives to Geneva for a joint colloquium of the WHO and UNICEF, which concluded that breast-feeding was a vital activity. Two years later, the league secured the status of consultant to UNICEF and worked to make breast-feeding a global health issue.

What is noteworthy is how the recommendation to mothers in developing countries to breast-feed was extended to the rest of the world, and how it became increasingly dictatorial and restrictive. In line with the goals of the league and its medical supporters, major international organizations began to highlight the damaging effects of formula in industrialized countries. Unquestioningly accepting the claims of inferior health in bottle-fed children, advocates failed to differentiate between the general health of a baby born in the Sudan and one born in Paris. Down with formula!

In 1981, 118 member states of the WHO passed a resolution to restrict the marketing of breast-milk substitutes. It was recommended that advertising and the distribution of free samples be banned, and that any information about formula feeding mention that breast-feeding was better for the baby and include warnings about the risks and costs of using formula.[36] As Dr. Viviane Antony-Nebout pointed out: "Having been a subject of interest to doctors and industrial corporations, baby food moved into the realm of diplomats and UN committees." The worldwide goal stipulated exclusive breast-feeding for the first six months (no additional water, fruit juice or herbal infusions) and supplemented breast-feeding until at least the age of two.[37]

Faced with the inertia of some countries, such as France, international organizations called for more robust action. They turned to the United Nations Convention on the Rights of the Child (adopted on November 20, 1989), particularly Article 24,[38] and asked each government to establish legislative, judicial, and administrative measures to support breast-feeding. On August 1, 1990, thirty governments, along with the WHO, UNICEF, and various non-government organizations, signed the Innocenti Declaration, which reaffirmed the WHO's ideal length of time to breast-feed. Among the proposals to achieve this ideal was the appointment in each country of a national breast-feeding coordinator and committee; a directive that all maternity wards follow the WHO/UNICEF's recommendations[39] for successful breast-feeding; implementation of the international code for the marketing of breast-milk substitutes; and protection of working mothers' rights to breast-feed their children.

A year later,[40] the WHO and UNICEF launched the Baby-Friendly Hospital Initiative: hospitals and maternity wards that instituted specific Innocenti recommendations would receive an internationally recognized "Baby Friendly" designation. Since then, global organizations and associations have put continuous pressure on governments to implement the WHO/UNICEF directives. For its part, the EU twice (in 2004 and 2008) set up programs to promote and facilitate breast-feeding both politically and financially. The aim was to inform the public about breast-feeding and train health professionals to encourage mothers in the practice, and also to assess and monitor the nursing success rate.

There is no denying that the La Leche League has won the ideological battle.[41] With the support of major international organizations, the league succeeded in convincing politicians and institutions of the superior benefits of breast-feeding. But for all that, have mothers themselves been convinced to breast-feed exclusively for six months and then continue with supplemented breast-feeding until the child is two?

THE BALANCE SHEET

Overall, Western countries have seen breast-feeding rates rise since the 1970s. Today the majority of women—virtually all women in some countries—breast-feed during their time in the maternity ward. Under close surveillance from nurses (or family), it is almost impossible not to. On the other hand, once mothers return home, the period of continued breast-feeding varies a great deal from one country to another and depends on the mother's sociocultural circumstances.

Spectacular Results

In North America, breast-feeding has made significant gains, but these are still deemed inadequate by pro-breast-feeding associations. In the United States, only 26 percent of mothers spent any time breast-feeding in the 1970s. In 1982, the figure had risen to 62 percent and in 2011 to 75 percent. Only fourteen states, however, reached the federal government's target of 60.6 percent of mothers still breast-feeding at six months, while the national average stood at 44 percent.

In fifteen states, 25 percent of women breast-fed for twelve months, compared to 22.4 percent nationally.[42]

In Quebec the increase is on a similar scale. At the beginning of the 1970s, only 5 percent of Quebec women breast-fed for six months.[43] By 2010, 84 percent of women began breast-feeding while in the maternity ward, and 22 percent still exclusively breast-fed at six months. In 2001, a survey by the Australian Bureau of Statistics showed that 87 percent of Australian children aged 0–3 years had been breast-fed at some point. By the age of six months, the percentage of infants being breast-fed stood at 48 percent; this dropped off to 23 percent for children around one year of age.[44]

In Europe the statistics vary considerably from one country to another. In 2002, Scandinavians were at the top of the class, while the failures were the French, as the following tables show.[45]

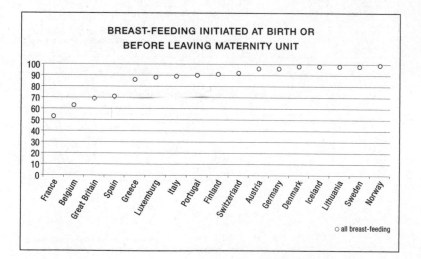

BREAST-FEEDING INITIATED AT BIRTH OR BEFORE LEAVING MATERNITY UNIT

○ all breast-feeding

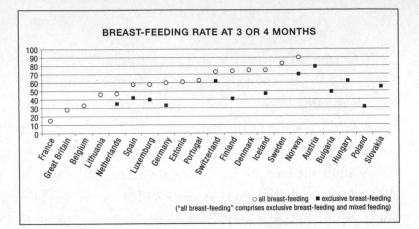

BREAST-FEEDING RATE AT 3 OR 4 MONTHS

○ all breast-feeding ■ exclusive breast-feeding
("all breast-feeding" comprises exclusive breast-feeding and mixed feeding)

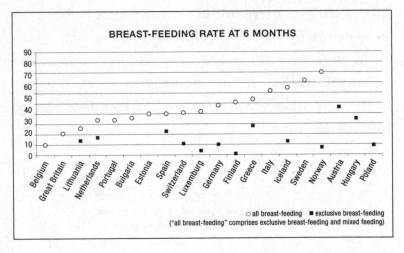

BREAST-FEEDING RATE AT 6 MONTHS

○ all breast-feeding ■ exclusive breast-feeding
("all breast-feeding" comprises exclusive breast-feeding and mixed feeding)

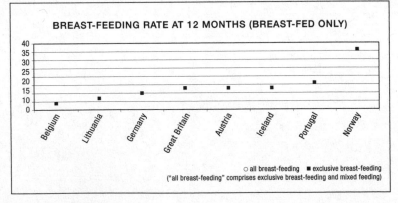

BREAST-FEEDING RATE AT 12 MONTHS (BREAST-FED ONLY)

○ all breast-feeding ■ exclusive breast-feeding
("all breast-feeding" comprises exclusive breast-feeding and mixed feeding)

In Sweden and Norway, the breast-feeding rate has shown a spectacular U curve since the 1950s.[46] The trough was in the years 1972–1973, when just 30 percent of Swedish women breast-fed at two months and 6 percent at six months, while in Norway, only 5 percent still breast-fed at six months. Since 1993–1994, the rate has risen continuously.[47] In 2010, 99 percent of babies in Norway were breast-fed when they left the maternity ward; for Swedish babies, the figure was 98 percent, and the Finnish statistics are similar.[48] Babies in Scandinavian countries are also breast-fed the longest. Only the Austrians (93 percent)[49] bear comparison, although the rates for Spain, Poland, Romania, and the Czech Republic are all above 90 percent.[50]

To explain this quasi unanimity in Scandinavian countries, the International Pediatric Association[51] cites a combination of factors: very active pro-breast-feeding organizations supported by political cooperation at the highest level. "Rather than representing breast-feeding as a duty for women, it is by claiming it as a right that mothers have reestablished how natural breast-feeding is. . . . This right is associated with another, the right to benefit from adequate maternity leave and a re-adaptation to the world of work."[52]

Anyone can appreciate the significance of the positive shift from a "duty" to a "right."

But a doubt remains: What does this unanimity mean within a democracy? If breast-feeding is a right, then is not breast-feeding also a right? Are Norwegian and Swedish women able to exercise their freedom of choice and refuse to conform to this moral and social norm? The notion of 100 percent of women wanting to breast-feed is as troubling as 100 percent of women not wanting to do so.

Bad Mothers

Ireland and France are at the bottom of the class, the shame of breast-feeding Europe. In 1999, only Irish women seemed to perform worse than the French: 45 percent[53] against 60 percent breast-fed at birth. However, as Ireland rarely provides statistics, French women are the ones who usually bear the brunt of failure. And yet French organizations advocating breast-feeding are far from inactive, and support from the press increases with each passing year. The French La Leche League, set up in 1973, now has close to 200 local branches.[54] It publishes two quarterly reviews[55] and, in addition to Co-Naître, which promotes natural childbirth and breast-feeding, contributes to training health professionals. Its militant stance has borne fruit, judging by the growth curve in breast-feeding rates at birth: 40.5 percent in 1995, 55.4 percent in 2003, and 60.2 percent in 2010.[56]

Granted, French women who choose to breast-feed are still fewer than other European countries, but the figures are rising. The real blot on their record is that French women still breast-feed for a hopelessly short time. Only 42 percent of babies are breast-fed after eight weeks (compared to 86 percent at three months in Norway).[57] To put it bluntly, French mothers balk at playing the role expected of them, and successive governments over the last thirty years have dragged their feet in bringing the country into line with the WHO requirements conveyed by European guidelines. It took more than seventeen years[58] for France to implement the international code for marketing breast-milk substitutes. And unlike Great Britain, it did not sign the 1990 Innocenti Declaration.

Weary of this political inertia, associations that offer breast-feeding support and information came together in 2000 to form a new organization, COFAM,[59] the French Committee for Breast-feeding Mothers, to fill the role of national coordinator. COFAM organizes the annual World Breast-feeding Day, facilitates dialogue between professionals and associations, and circulates a great many brochures. It oversees the Baby-Friendly Hospital Initiative and has obtained support from the Ministry of Health. In 2001, the member associations succeeded in including breast-feeding as one of nine objectives of France's first National Nutrition and Health Policy. In the second policy, launched in 2006, the objective was to increase exclusive breast-feeding at birth from 56 percent to 70 percent.

The battle is still not over, however. According to Antony-Nebout, "There is a general lack of determination to allocate sufficient funds to initiatives that favor breast-feeding mothers, and in particular to the Baby-Friendly Hospital Initiative."[60] Although there were 20,000 Baby-Friendly Hospitals globally in 2007, with 650 in Europe, France at that time was lagging in last place, with only five[61] as shown by the table below drawn up from 2007 UNICEF figures.[62] Even Ireland was doing better.

The indifference at the government level is a clear reflection of the indifference of French society in general and, more particularly, of French women. Until relatively recently, breast-feeding was presented as a choice, a right, and a pleasure. But in the absence of satisfactory results, breast-feeding promoters have stepped up efforts to make women feel guilty. Now the rhetoric tends to be more vigorous. There is less talk of a right and more of a duty. The National Academy of Medicine is now fiercely in favor of feeding newborns at the breast.[64] The message is clear: a good mother breast-feeds. Significantly, this good mother shares a sociocultural profile with women in other developed countries: she is over thirty, is a high-earning professional, does not smoke, takes pre-natal classes, and benefits from long maternity leave.[65]

Unspoken Resistance

There are many women who resist the breast-feeding trend, but they go unheard or underground. In developed countries, only a rare few would risk challenging the need to breast-feed,

	number of BFH	% of all maternity wards	% of national number of births
Australia[63]	74	23	33
Austria	14	13	
Belgium	6		9.7
Bulgaria	5	4.5	10
Denmark	11	33	22
France	5	0.7	
Germany	18	1.8	
Hungary	9	8	
Ireland	3	14	17
Italy	8	1	1.5
Lithuania	6	12	
Luxemburg	2	33	35
Macedonia	28	97	
Netherlands	38	20	35
Norway	36	64	77
Poland	52	11	
Romania	10	5.5	12
Russia	162	5	13
Spain	52	100	100
Switzerland	59	40	55
United Kingdom	43	16	16

and it takes a lot of nerve for a newly delivered mother to defy instructions from nurses and doctors. Rare too are the medical experts who make a clear distinction between the proven benefits of breast-feeding and the many other claims suggested by various studies but subsequently disproved.[66] A 2005 report by the French Society of Pediatrics emphasized: "On condition that it is exclusive and lasts more than three months, breast-feeding reduces the incidence and gravity of digestive, ENT, and respiratory infections. This is the primary benefit of breast-feeding and is responsible for a reduction in morbidity and mortality in breast-fed babies, including those in industrialized countries."[67]

However, these broad claims for the benefits of breast-feeding were challenged in an article published in the October 2007 issue of the *British Medical Journal*. In a sweeping study of 17,046 Belorussian infants carried out over six years, Michael Kramer of Canada's McGill University concluded that breast-feeding does not offer greater protection against asthma or allergies, contrary to what we have been repeatedly told.

The French Society of Pediatrics had gone one step further, linking breast-feeding to cognitive development. A year earlier, UK statistician Geoff Der[68] published a much-discussed study on the subject, along with the IQs of more than five thousand children and their three thousand mothers, and concluded that there was absolutely no link between the two. By observing families in which one child had been breast-fed and the other not (particularly in the case of twins), he confirmed that the key factor contributing to the child's IQ was the mother's IQ, and that breast-feeding had no influence.[69] These striking results have done nothing to stop breast-feeding activists from allowing us to believe the contrary.[70]

Linda Blum, an American sociologist, is one of the few who dared to suggest that the advantages of breast-feeding in developed countries had been exaggerated; that a good many alleged benefits were far from established and required further research; and that formula was constantly being improved to reproduce the advantages of breast milk.[71] These iconoclastic words drew little attention in the media. At present, bottle-feeding is viewed as a necessary evil and is synonymous with a selfish mother.

It is hard to know what women really think about breast-feeding when they keep their feelings of ambivalence to themselves. In France, it seems possible to identify three categories of mothers. For some, breast-feeding is self-evident and an incomparably fulfilling and happy experience. They tend to find breast-feeding easy and succeed at it almost instantly. They breast-feed for more than two months and, if they return to work, use breast pumps. Although some would have us believe that all mothers, with the right advice, can achieve the same results, the women in this category are a minority.

At the other end of the spectrum are the 40 percent of

French mothers who refuse even to try breast-feeding. They are not tempted by the image of a nursing mother, nor by the prospect of caring for their baby one-on-one, round the clock. But given how hard it is to withstand being called monstrously selfish, it is likely that, as the pressure mounts, more women will try to breast-feed, at least while they are in the hospital.

The third category of women start breast-feeding in the hospital and stop soon after returning home. They rarely talk about not wanting to nurse or even feeling repelled by the idea. They instead put their decision down to exhaustion, or a poor milk supply, or the agony of cracked nipples, or the hours waiting for the baby to be sated. These mothers tried, but breast-feeding didn't work for them. Activists chorus in reply that none of these reasons is acceptable: every woman can breast-feed. A mother's ambivalence is of no consequence.

A few advocates of breast-feeding do recognize that mothers might feel trapped by political correctness and they challenge the movement's sentimental image of motherhood with its erasure of all the other aspects of breast-feeding: the loss of freedom and the despotism of an insatiable child. They recognize that a baby might be a source of happiness, but also a devastating tornado. On-demand breast-feeding can leave women feeling like "a walking meal"[72] or a "giant pacifier"[73] or a milk-producing "ecosystem," of having lost their status as individuals with their own will and desires.[74] But these cries do not appear in the pro-breast-feeding literature, which claims that what is good for some is good for all. Even though psychologists[75] object to the concept of innate mothering and the illusion of harmony between mother and baby, there is no place for such subtleties. The underlying commandment of the dominant new ideology is "Mothers, you owe them everything!"

4

THE BABY'S DOMINION

The irony of this history is that it was precisely at the point that Western women finally rid themselves of patriarchy that they acquired a new master in the home. Women had achieved financial independence as well as control over whether they had children or not: they had no reason, it seemed, to continue to confront men's power.

Yet, thirty years later, there is no denying that male domination persists. Men's general resistance to the model of equality is indisputable, but this alone does not explain women's situation today. Their increased responsibility for babies and young children has proved just as restrictive, if not more so, than sexism in the home or in the workplace. A woman might be able to turn her back on her boss or her husband, but she can hardly walk a way from her baby.

The tyranny of maternal duty is not new, but it has become considerably more pronounced with the rise of naturalism, and it has thus far produced neither a matriarchy nor sexual equality, but rather a regression in women's status. We have agreed to this regression in the name of moral superiority, the love we bear for our children, and some ideal notion of child rearing, all of which are proving far more effective than external constraints. As everyone knows, there is nothing quite like voluntary servitude. And men have not had to lift a finger to accomplish this fall. The best allies of men's dominance have been, quite unwittingly, innocent infants.

THE MOTHER BEFORE THE FATHER

It seems a long time ago that we were grateful for baby bottles because they promised that men and women could share parenting from birth. In France, where 40 percent of couples use bottles from birth, there is still significant resistance to the new orthodoxy. We should be thankful to Laurence Pernoud, the queen of French parenting guides, for championing the right to choose between breast- and bottle-feeding.[1] Bottles, she said, give fathers the opportunity for additional contact with the baby and offer mothers some relief. This approval will seem heretical to the ayatollahs of breast-feeding, whose concept of parents' roles is very traditional, even with their patina of modernity. The La Leche

League claims: "The father should support and encourage the mother to breastfeed her baby completely." The league does also urge the father to "give more time to family life than professional success, spend more time with his child, and take on his fair share of domestic tasks."[2] The idea was repeated almost verbatim by such media-friendly pediatricians as T. Berry Brazelton in the United States and Edwige Antier in Paris.

In the 1960s and 1970s, thanks to bottle-feeding, young couples experimented with sharing roles, which was more conducive to the mother's freedom, allowing her to leave the house, sleep through the night, perhaps even go back to her work without anxiety. Feeding fathers, whom the French sometimes called "father hens," played a not insignificant role in women's liberation by helping mothers juggle family and work life.[3] There might not have been legions of them, they might have come in for plenty of teasing, and the media might have exaggerated their prevalence, but they managed to change the image of the traditional father. Giving the baby a bottle and bath, changing diapers—all these "women's" jobs could be done by men, without undermining their virility or the mothers' commitment to their children. But interchangeable roles were incompatible with the tenets of breast-feeding and the notion of maternal instinct.

From the middle of the 1990s, when breast-feeding returned to prominence in France, new fathers were shot down and their role redefined.[4] From Edwige Antier:

While the ideology that favors "new fathers" quite rightly emphasizes how important fathers are in caring for the baby, I am keen to point out that a father's role is far from that of a second mother. . . . A baby does not dream of having two mothers, but to curl up in his mother's arms and feel that his father is wrapping both of them in his protective presence. We must, at all costs, stop trying to convert fathers into mothering fathers. This *current trend* is utterly *ridiculous and laughable. A father's role is to protect the mother, to increase her standing* as a mother and as a woman. Both must have their own place. For a child, the best sort of daddy is one who loves and protects . . . Mommy![5]

The father should be present in the first months to free the mother from domestic chores, to play with the baby, to "reintroduce the mother to her femininity" by "giving her flowers, babysitting while she goes to the hairdresser, telling her how lovely she looks."[6] Breast-feeding exclusively for the first six months essentially excludes the father from the mother-child couple. He is only in the way. He has no place interfering in this intense relationship. If the father wants to bottle-feed his baby, he should be told that it is unnecessary. Its only effect is to "soothe . . . the father."[7]

The mother who breast-feeds on demand day and night, Antier says, has to be "completely available." She therefore concludes, positively, that in "the early months, a mother is

a slave to her baby."[8] As supplemental breast-feeding is recommended until the age of two, it will be quite a while
before the ideal mother recovers her freedom. And so the
model of the patriarchal couple is restored. After twenty
years of militant feminism, fathers have now been given
justification for not being totally fascinated by their newborn babies. With the baby back to being exclusively the
mother's concern, the father is once again free to attend to
his own affairs with a clear conscience.

If we add to this the fact that Antier, like devotees of the
La Leche League, strongly recommends that mothers stay
at home with their children until the age of three, they can
bid farewell to their professional ambitions. If, in the process,
a woman has another child, we can safely say that Mommy
has come home for good.

Scandinavian countries are fiercely militant about breast-
feeding but more sensitive than anywhere else about sexual
equality. They have launched unprecedented family policies
that aim to prevent mothers of young children being penal-
ized in the job market.

As early as 1974, Olof Palme's government in Sweden
replaced maternity leave with parental leave to be shared
between the mother and father. Now parental leave can be
spread over a total of sixteen months for a couple, thirteen
of which are indemnified at 80 percent salary, and three
months at a flat rate, with a ceiling of around $3,500 a
month. The father must take at least two months of the

leave, otherwise this time is deducted from the total period allocated. Additional paternity leave was added in 1980, giving fathers the right to an extra ten days paid at 80 percent salary.[9] This bold policy to integrate parents equally in their children's upbringing did not prompt huge upheavals. Nearly 80 percent of fathers use all or part of their paternity leave, but they take only about 22 percent of the total compensated parental leave days in the country."[10]

If we look more closely, therefore, it seems far from certain that Swedish policies, which are held up as a model to the rest of the world, have managed to reconcile motherhood and sexual equality, or even to contain the salary gap between men and women.

THE BABY BEFORE THE COUPLE

Whether she is married or in a relationship, a mother is expected to put her baby before the father.

Day and night, on-demand breast-feeding, as recommended, has two consequences that are far from conducive to a good relationship. The mother's breasts belong to the baby for months on end, and so does her bed. Among its other campaigns, the La Leche League launched a crusade for co-sleeping, which is deemed beneficial to the baby. It is not just that "co-sleeping and breastfeeding go well together,"[11] but co-sleeping offers many advantages for the child. He is less wakeful or restless, Antier tells us, when he sleeps in his parents' bed: "He needs to hear his mother moving and his father snoring: it stimulates his attention span and improves his breathing pattern. To deprive your child of the reassurance offered by co-sleeping will damage his psychological development. To leave a baby crying when he is going to sleep or waking up is an extremely cruel practice, at least until the age of four."[12]

Apart from the psychological benefits, co-sleeping is claimed to prevent other problems: "The baby sleeps better, the mother and baby no longer wake each other up, the frequency and duration of nursing during the night increases. As well as greater physical contact between mother and baby, there is greater vigilance on the part of the mother. Without her realizing it or even fully waking up, she checks that her child is all right, is not too cold or hot, puts on or takes off a blanket, etc."[13] Co-sleeping proponents like to cite a 1996 study in New Zealand that showed a 25 percent reduced risk of SIDS (sudden infant death syndrome) in babies who slept in their parents' bedroom up to the age of six months.

But sleeping in the parents' room does not mean sleeping in their bed, a practice that, according to an article in the Lancet in 2004, actually increases the risk of SIDS—a conclusion that is contested by the champions of co-sleeping.[14]

Even if we accept the advantages of co-sleeping for the mother, who is spared having to get up several times in the night to breast-feed, the benefits for a child of three or four are uncertain. Child psychologists are divided. Some claim that it is common practice in many civilizations and entails no negative consequences. French child psychologist Marcel Rufo, originally hostile to the idea, eventually supported it as a short-term soothing practice for the baby. Others strongly oppose it. Claude Halmos, for example, thinks the baby needs the proximity of his mother's gentleness and the sound of her voice more than intense physical contact.

Rufo and Halmos both point out the dangers co-sleeping poses to the couple's relationship. Rufo worries that it drives the father out of the conjugal bed, exiling him to the living room, while Halmos argues that a child who sleeps next to his mother is "part of a system where the notion of his parents as a couple, separate from him, does not feature. He is, therefore, not in his rightful place."[15]

These reservations leave co-sleeping advocates unmoved. In the words of Edwige Antier: "Plenty of fathers do not mind the baby sleeping in their double bed. As for sexual desire, it is often slower to return in the mother, who is so wrapped up in her child. But it will return all the stronger if she feels she is understood by her husband, who helps her gain confidence in her abilities as a mother, reassures her about her powers of seduction, helps her regain her figure, gives her flowers . . . and continues to take her in his arms, baby included, to help her sleep." She concluded: "It is a difficult period in life, but a short one. If fathers are told that the more their baby nurses on demand, the more likely he is to be bright, this will give them the strength to bide their time."[16]

Bide their time: For how long? As we know, giving birth causes great changes in a woman's body, which, for physiological and psychological reasons, distance her from her sexuality. The physiological factors disappear with time, but the psychological barriers can sometimes be more difficult to overcome.

A child can turn the parents' connection completely upside down. There is no greater antithesis to the couple as lovers than the couple as parents. Even if they do not sleep with their child, it is hard to switch from one role to the other. If the woman breast-feeds for months, even years, how are the couple to retain intimacy and sexuality? The challenge is that much greater with the difficulty of distinguishing the breast-feeding breast from the sexual breast. A breast-feeding mother experiences pleasure, but she is not necessarily an object of desire for the father watching her. And there are plenty of young mothers who admit that their relationship with their baby is enough, that they have no desire to resume sexual activity. So the woman-as-mother may well obliterate the woman-as-lover and endanger the couple.

This theme appears several times in Éliette Abécassis's novel, most notably during a La Leche League group meeting:

> "My baby sleeps with me. Actually, I've even asked my partner to sleep in the living room because there isn't enough room for the three of us."

"About time too!" [the other members reply in unison].
"Would you like to share your experience with us?"

"My experience. Since having a baby, I've stopped having a relationship, I've stopped sleeping, I've stopped washing my hair, I've stopped reading and I've stopped
seeing my friends. I've become a mother, okay. But I
didn't know that a mother was just a mother. I didn't
realize you had to give up all the other parts you play,
give up on sexuality, seduction, work, sports, your own
body, your own mind. I didn't know you had to give up
on life."

All eyes turn to me as if I am a murderer, or worse, a
bad mother.[17]

The heroine goes back to La Leche League meetings several times and changes, becoming a good mother who plans
her life around breast-feeding:

It gave me so much satisfaction, the pleasure in giving was
so intense, so intimate, so complete, that I didn't need
anything else. I didn't need to make love with my partner
anymore. . . . I lived off those moments of peace when
what I wanted and what the baby wanted were the same
thing, and I ended up giving him the breast because I
wanted to, giving it to him the way you make love, and
finding I felt whole again, like I had before, a very long
time ago.[18]

The couple in this novel never recovers, ultimately splitting up. The extremity of this experience is not the rule, far from it. Some might say that this fictional couple must have been fairly unstable anyway, if they were unable to rekindle their desire. But even in real life, the patience of the father is not the answer to a mother's immersion in her child: a mother cannot allow herself to be consumed by her baby to the point of destroying her desires as a woman. The devotees of extreme mothering have nothing to say on this score. Only the mother exists because only the child matters. The couple's stability and the importance of the sexuality that cements it go unmentioned.[19] There is in this dynamic more than a whiff of centuries past, when the couple's relationship was based not on love, and come what may, marriages did not end. This ideal of family life profoundly contradicts the aspirations of most men and women in the twenty-first century.

THE CHILD BEFORE THE WOMAN

The 1970s were characterized by women's clarion call of "Me first!"[20] It was a call aimed primarily at men, but also at their children. Mothers told their personal stories: they were encouraged to express themselves on the great taboo subject of maternal ambivalence and even on their feelings of alienation from their babies.[21] Books and confessions poured out, publicly voicing what today is confided solely to the psychologist.[22] Even if those voices constituted only a minority, they nonetheless stripped motherhood of its sanctity, gave new life to women's desires, and banished feelings of guilt from the silent sufferers who found no reward in child rearing.

Milk and Time

Advocating on-demand breast-feeding for as long as the child wants it effectively deprives a mother of her time. If you add to this the obligation to stay by his side until the age of three to optimize his development, she receives the message that any other interest is secondary and morally inferior, since the ideal mother is enmeshed with her child bodily and mentally. The fact that this model is unavailable to a good many women who cannot afford the luxury of staying at home and undesirable to plenty of others has not silenced its boosters, in both public opinion and individual practice.

An ideological turning point occurred in 1990 among the generation of women who were then in their twenties. The daughters of feminists, militant or otherwise, they proceeded to engage in a classic settling of accounts with their mothers. After thanking them for winning the right to contraception and abortion, the daughters then demanded an admission of failure. Their accusation to their mothers could be summarized thus: You sacrificed everything for your independence and you ended up with twice as much work. You were underrated in the workplace and spent too little time at home; you lost out on all fronts. They did not intend to repeat their mothers' mistakes.

The daughters also rejected the "feminist" label, as if it cast women in a bad light. Indeed, some among the new generation embraced the most clichéd male stereotypes of feminism, associating it with hysteria, aggression, carnality, and man-hating. The judgment was final: feminism had passed its sell-by date.

Beneath this rejection of feminism lurked a deeper criticism of motherhood as their mothers had practiced it. Perhaps they really meant: In pursuit of your independence, you sacrificed me as well. You didn't give me enough love, enough care, enough time. You were always in a hurry and often tired; you thought the quality of the time you spent with me was more important than the quantity. The truth is, I was not your top priority and you were not a good mother. I won't do the same with my children.

Unfair or not, this condemnation of mothers by their daughters is common and widely recognized in psychoanalysis. But now, for the first time, the mothers being criticized were precisely the ones who had fought for women's independence. As the daughters became mothers themselves, they talked less about their freedom and personal ambitions, or even about equal pay. They put these claims on the back burner while they gave priority to their children. At the same time, there was more talk of how important it was to "nego-tiate" a work-family balance and "reconcile" time spent at work with time spent as a mother.

This change in attitudes, which took place during an economic crisis, was accelerated by the mass unemployment affecting all Western countries. In France, paid parental leave[23] was increased in 1994, prompting a significant with-drawal from the workplace by mothers of young children, particularly among those with the least qualifications. At the other end of the social scale, highly qualified women, especially those in liberal professions, also retreated to the home when they became mothers. In 2003, the *New York Times*[24] announced that we were witnessing an "opt-out rev-olution," a move on the part of professional women to leave work and stay at home with their children.[25] More often than not, these women had partners who were able to meet their family's needs comfortably; for single mothers and divorcées there is no such choice.

It is too early to know whether these new patterns con-stitute a genuine revolution. For now, the statistics for work-ing women have remained fairly stable. On the other hand, the idea that women can simultaneously be good mothers and pursue impressive careers is under attack. It is true that there has been a significant rise in women working part-time. Many mothers choose to work fewer hours to fit the criteria of a good mother, but a large number of women have had part-time work imposed on them by the shrinking workplace. Either way, the result is that the salary gap between men and women has remained the same, if not grown slightly wider.

Another Look at the Swedish Model

No one doubts that Sweden has made considerable efforts to reconcile motherhood with a career and create conditions for equality in the workplace. On top of the parental leave that absorbs 40 percent of the country's family policies budget, flexible working hours for both parents of children under eight,[26] and time off to care for sick children, Sweden also offers state day care.[27] In sum, the Swedish model is in the vanguard of European family policies.

With what results?

As we have seen, fathers take only one-fifth of the parental leave available. As for mothers, 80 percent return to work, but two in five opt for part-time jobs.[28] When Catherine Hakim published *Key Issues in Women's Work*[29] in 1996, she revealed that Swedish family policies were not as conducive to sexual equality as was previously believed. They were favorable to raising the birthrate but considerably less so to advancing women's careers. Studying all the usual criteria for measuring equality in the workplace, Hakim showed that Sweden was barely faring any better than England or France.

Looking at salaries, Hakim cites findings that 80 percent of Swedish women are paid below a given threshold, while

80 percent of men were paid above it. One reason for the divide was that two-thirds of Swedish women worked in the public sector, while 75 percent of men worked in the more difficult and demanding private sector. According to Hakim, the more the state extended its family policies, the less inclined private companies were to hire women because, they claimed, they could not afford such generous maternity leave. On top of this, the glass ceiling was no less cruel in Sweden than elsewhere. Hakim's data showed that women comprised only 1.5 percent of top management at a time when that figure was at 11 percent in the United States. However by 2010, that figure, measured by the number of women in executive committees, had reached 14 percent in the United States and 17 percent in Sweden.[30]

As for the salary gap between men and women (the ultimate criterion for sexual equality), Hakim highlighted the fact that in countries with less generous family policies, the salary gap tended to be smaller. This remains true: in 2009, Swedish women across the board were paid around 16 percent less than Swedish men, comparable to France and Spain.[31] In the same year, the pay gap in Australia was around 17 percent.[32] In Italy, by contrast, the gap in 2009 was only 5.5 percent; in Belgium 9, and in Poland 10 percent. (Hakim omits to point out that the birthrate has dropped dramatically in Italy.)

To date, no family policy has proved truly effective at improving equality between men and women. The division of work between a couple is still unequal in every country, including Scandinavia. The increasingly onerous responsibilities placed on mothers just aggravate the situation. Only fully sharing parental roles from birth could counter this trend, yet in the name of our children's well-being we are taking the opposite route. Sexist men can celebrate: we will not see the end of their reign anytime soon. They have won a war without taking up arms, and without having said a word. The champions of maternalism took care of it all.

PART THREE

OVERLOADING THE BOAT

Every culture subscribes to an a ideal of motherhood, although it might vary with the times. Whether or not they are aware of it, all women are influenced by that ideal. They might accept or avoid it, negotiate with or reject it, but ultimately their choices are made in relation to it.

Today's ideal is supremely demanding, even more than twenty years ago, when people had already begun to register the expanding demands made of mothers. As American sociologist Michelle Stanworth noted, "Mothering involves responsibility not only for the physical and emotional care of children, but for detailed attention to their psychological, social and intellectual development. Motherhood is seen, more than in the past, as a full-time occupation. Mothers may be expected now to lavish as much 'care' on two children as they might previously have provided for six."[1] However, today's ideal of a woman is different from that of a mother. Personal fulfillment has become the driving motivation of our time. Women thus find themselves caught in a multiple contradiction.

The first of these is social. While boosters of the traditional family condemn working mothers, companies resent them for their children. For many, motherhood is held as the highest form of fulfillment for women even as yet it is devalued socially. Full-time mothers are unpaid, suspected of doing nothing all day, and deprived of a professional identity because their work requires no qualifications. In a society where most people work and ideal women have successful careers, anyone who stays at home or puts her children first risks being dismissed as insignificant.

The second contradiction is conjugal. Couples tend to expect and desire children, yet, as many have noted, a child is not conducive to a couple's love life. Exhaustion, lack of sleep and intimacy, and the constraints and sacrifices imposed by a child can get the better of a couple. Many partners separate in the first three years after a child is born. A good number of young couples admit that they only realized the demands of the job after the fact[2] ("no one warned me," they say). Increasingly, partners are taking a hard second look before launching on this adventure.

The most painful contradiction lies is personal, affecting every woman who does not identify fully with motherhood, every woman who feels torn between love for her child and personal desires, between wanting the best for her baby and wanting the best for herself. A child conceived as a source of fulfillment can, it turns out, stand in the way of that fulfillment.[3] And, if we pile up a mother's responsibilities to the point of overload, she will feel this contradiction all the more keenly.

These contradictions are rarely given serious consideration. And by expecting ever more of mothers, the naturalist ideology not only fails to offer solutions, it makes the contradictions untenable. In different countries, of course, these contradictions differ in their degree of acuteness. There are two distinct tendencies, which vary according to how closely each country identifies women with mothers. Wherever the prevailing ideal conflates the two, women who cannot fulfill the expectations pinned on them are increasingly likely to turn their backs on motherhood. In countries where being a woman and being a mother are seen as distinct identities, where the legitimacy of multiple women's roles is recognized, and where motherhood does not overwhelm all other possibilities, women do want to have children, even if it means falling short of the ideal of motherhood.

5

THE DIVERSITY OF
WOMEN'S ASPIRATIONS

Women today are faced with a new question: What should I do to feel fulfilled? Is motherhood the most enriching experience available to me? Would I be more fulfilled by a career? If I don't want to sacrifice either possibility, to which should I give priority? For most women, a life without children is unthinkable, but they do not wish to give up their financial independence, their social lives, and their means of self-affirmation. Over the last thirty years, women have planned to have children later and later in their lives. The average age at which women now have their first child is around thirty, once they have finished studying and training, found work, and met a stable partner. There are many preliminaries that involve putting off having a child until later, or, as it turns out, never. For some women, the decision to have children, as sociologist Pascale Donati has said, is not so much rejected as "inactivated."[1] For those rare others, children are simply out of the question.

THE WOMAN AS MOTHER

Vocational Motherhood

Women who find motherhood wholly fulfilling often talk about themselves in terms of instinct. Journalist Pascale Pontoreau wrote:

> I wanted to have children quickly. Lots of children. Every time I mentioned the insistent call of my maternal instinct my friends would tease me. Before long I began to feel that wanting children was some kind of compulsion, an irrational longing deep within me and very hard to explain. I had to set aside sober thinking to make way for pregnancy, and then for the enchantment of my adorable little girl. . . .
>
> The only thing that mattered was the deep, powerful, indestructible desire that carried me through to the end of my first pregnancy. It was autonomous, irrevocable, visceral. I realized that this longing for motherhood was not the result of a thought process. It had emerged instinctively.[2]

For women who feel this vocation, their fulfillment does not stop at intimacy with their newborn. The child becomes their life's work because he is a thrilling creation that nothing else can rival. Taking care of him, helping him develop from one milestone to the next, the joy and pride of seeing him become an adult—this is hardly an unambitious enterprise, quite the opposite. But for true fulfillment, which is never guaranteed, both the mother and the child must derive pleasure from the process. She has, after all, abandoned her work to become the "exclusive"[3] or "intensive"[4] mother recommended by the Brazeltons and Antiers of this world. The child's needs are the center of her universe, she invests deeply in him emotionally, and she is more than happy to devote all her time and energy to him.

These mothers do exist, but are they common? How many women stay at home to bring up a child and realize they have made a mistake by leaving their jobs? How many leave a monotonous job for a task they thought would be wonderful but turns out to be depressing? Some women might admit to their closest friends that they feel drained or crazy. But how could they know exclusive motherhood would feel like this until they had tried it? And how can they admit to having making the wrong choice?

Nullipara[5]

Then there are women who do have a vocation for motherhood but are unable to have children. How do they manage to get over their loss? Whether chosen or imposed, being without children, which is what differentiates women from mothers, is a state that connotes deficiency and incompleteness. Some women claim that state deliberately; others never recover from it. Involuntary childlessness leaves many women feeling severed from their essence and from their place in the world. Novelist Jane Sautière expressed this in her novel *Nullipara*:

> Nullipara. The first thing I hear is that empty sound, "nul." But there is also "para," the Greek for "beside," which to me means "sidelined." A women who is nullipara will always be on the sidelines, will never be part of something. It sounds so much like "nulle part," which means "nowhere." A woman from nowhere, inadmissible on the grounds of her origins (and in case we forget, it is always the origins that the offspring want to know about), an empty place and an emptier woman wandering over it.[6]

Of course, infertility might not be the reason for this childless woman's sorrow. The vagaries of life, circumstantial events, missed opportunities—these all might have made the decision for her. Some scholars[7] are dubious about personal explanations for this kind of childlessness, arguing that the cause ultimately always lies with social and economic factors. Although this socioeconomic view offers a rather limited understanding of a woman's motives, it does nonetheless help shed light on the murkier aspects of unrealized motherhood. But whatever interpretations of child-lessness psychologists and sociologists might suggest, surely the bottom line is that having a child was not the highest priority and the woman in question did not identify with motherhood as closely as she might think.

Infertile women (or couples) are in quite a different situation, yet they, like people who do not want children, are all too often the target of criticism. They are all equally suspect. Those who can't have children are expected to put up with it nobly, while those who do not want them are condemned as selfish, irresponsible, somehow impaired. One way or the other, their lot is public disapproval and their sentence is psychoanalysis, either to help them get over it—that is, accept their "abnormal" fate—or to get comfortable with the norm and comply with expectations. Who cares whether the infertile woman might have made an exceptional mother, while the other one, the woman who does not want children, might have been a dreadful one? No one asks this question; our society prefers not to examine such subtleties.

FROM REFUSAL TO POSTPONEMENT

Over the last twenty years, an increasing number of women have chosen to opt out of motherhood. The phenomenon is not in fact new: a hundred years ago, a large proportion of women did not have children[8]—those in holy orders, those too poor to marry, servants. They formed the ranks of the childless, a fate that was often endured rather than chosen. Today we understand the phenomenon differently, not only because women have far greater freedom to choose mother-hood or not but because they also have other possible and desirable choices, which means that their fate is no longer synonymous with motherhood. Some women have always felt that they have a choice; others realize it at some point in their lives; still others are surprised to realize that they never grasped or exercised their ability to choose.

Saying No to Children

In France, almost a third of women who do not have chil-dren say they made a deliberate choice.[9] This minority has been called the "early articulators." Within this group, there are people who admit to simply not liking children (some-thing that could hardly be voiced until recently), people who claim to be acting in the interest of the child, and people who have put their own desires first.

Philosopher Michel Onfray, a strong advocate against marriage and having children, gives voice to the notion of remaining childless for the sake of the child. His position is rooted in a moral hedonism:

> Children, who in the first place never actually ask to be born, are entitled to expect not only material support from their parents, but also psychological, ethical, intellectual, cultural

and spiritual support for at least the first two decades of life. Since father- and motherhood are not ethical imperatives but metaphysical options, the urge to bring life into the world must absolutely be backed by the ability and intention to make that life as worthwhile as possible.[10]

To those who accuse childless people of selfishness, Onfray says that perhaps those who choose to have children are even more selfish:

People who choose not to have children love them just as much, if not more, than parents who are abundantly fruitful. Asked why he had abstained from producing an heir, Thalès de Millet replied: "Precisely because I love children. . . . Who truly finds reality sufficiently desirable to introduce their son or daughter to the inevitability of death, to the treachery of man's dealings with man, to the self-interest that fuels the world, to the burden of being forced to do tiring work for pay, if not to precarious unemployment? How could parents be so naïve, stupid and short-sighted as to love misery, illness, destitution, poverty, old age and misery enough to want to pass them on to their offspring? . . . Should we really use the word *love* to describe the transmission of such evils to the flesh of our flesh?"[11]

Those who have taken a rather more pragmatic and individualist position on not having children tend to talk directly in terms of personal fulfillment. They have made a choice to live their lives in a particular way, associating motherhood with burden and loss—of freedom, energy, money, pleasure, intimacy, and even identity. A child is synonymous with sacrifice and frustrating, even repellent, obligations; it is perhaps a threat to the stability and happiness of one's relationships.[12] These women have abortions if they become pregnant and sometimes choose to be sterilized.[13] They refer to themselves as "child-free" rather than childless because they are free of children and therefore of motherhood.

The Postponers

Most young women readily acknowledge that they would like to become mothers,[14] but motherhood is not their immediate priority. They feel they have plenty of time to make that choice and more pressing goals: to earn a living, create a home, build a career, find the right partner, and make the most of their freedom together. Once settled in a relationship, both partners need to make the decision to have a child; they both need to feel "ready."[15] If one of these goals is not reached, the decision is postponed. As Pascale Donati says, "Wanting children does not mean that the conditions for deciding to have one have been met."[16] The obstacle to constant postponement, however, is the woman's biological clock, which at some point puts an end to the process. A woman in her late thirties still has a 70 percent chance of being able to bear a child; in her early forties, the rate drops precipitously, to closer to 30 percent.

Canadian sociologist Jean E. Veevers, one of the first to do work related to couples known as "postponers,"[17] identified four stages in a progression from wanting children to not wanting to have them. In the first stage, the couple, or individual, gives priority to achieving a number of specific goals. In the second, they postpone the decision to an undetermined time: the couple is increasingly vague about the question and say they will have a child when they feel "more ready for it." The third stage is recognition, for the first time, of the possibility of not having children, and the beginning of discussions about the advantages and disadvantages of this choice. Finally, in the fourth stage, the couple decides to remain childless rather than disrupt their lives and relationship.[18] Veevers points out that in most cases the decision is not made explicitly. The process is acknowledged after the fact.

Women who enjoy fulfilling lives as part of a couple form only one group among the postponers. Others have never been in that position and find themselves postmenopausal and childless almost "by chance."[19] The range of experiences in this group varies widely: some women "neither want nor don't want children;" they put the question aside at first; it gradually fades or resurfaces "from time to time without ever materializing into a plan."[20] Other women definitely wanted to be mothers but did not meet the right man or met him too late; and some see themselves as victims of circumstances that stopped them from translating their wishes into reality.[21] Whether the reasons given are social, psychological, or economic, these postponers talk as if, in the absence of the foundation of marriage, imperceptible and uncontrollable forces have worked to reduce the chance of having children.

What is worth noting is that generally, the women in this group of voluntary postponers do not seem to be driven to act by maternal instinct. After all, a woman without a partner (or a willing partner) does have the option, in our age, of having a child alone, free from social stigma.

WOMAN AND MOTHER

In principle, most Western women want to be able to join their interests as women and their desire to be mothers. They want the means for their independence, a chance to establish themselves professionally, and fulfilling social lives and relationships. At the same time, they also want to experience motherhood, with all the love and joy that come with a child. These women do want to have it all.

To achieve this ideal, they are having children later, and fewer of them. But as soon as the first child is born, they find themselves having to negotiate between their two identities.

The Negotiators

These negotiations are made all the more difficult because the demands of both parts of women's lives are so great. Today's ideal of motherhood is at odds with the ever harsher pressures of the world of work. How is a woman to satisfy one realm without sacrificing the other? This question has been complicated over the last thirty years by a succession of economic crises and the threat of unemployment. And at the time, this was precisely the period when the ideal of the good mother became truly onerous.

A recent Australian study[22] by sociologists JaneMaree Maher and Lise Saugeres shows the extent to which commonly held views on motherhood can affect women's choices. Even though a good many mothers manage to negotiate with the ideal, all women, whether or not they have children, are influenced by at least certain of its aspects. In Australia, as in the United States and Great Britain, the model of "intensive" motherhood described by sociologist Sharon Hays,[23] whereby women are expected to be totally available to their children, holds considerable sway.

Maher and Saugeres argue that this cultural image of the good mother tends to be accepted at face value by women who do not have children, while those who do develop a less restrictive view of the subject. Unlike childless women, they often find they can reconcile their role as mothers and other personal goals. They might acknowledge the validity of the prevailing ideal, but the actual experience of motherhood demystifies the reality. According to Maher and Saugeres, there is "an increasing gap between how mothering is viewed and how it is practiced."[24]

The women interviewed for this study talk about motherhood as only a part of what they do and who they are. They are not unaware of the pressure to raise their children full-time, but most say they do not want to give in to it. Their identities as working women are not up for discussion. Thus they engage in negotiation.

The balance between these women's identities is fragile and unstable; the negotiations are never definitively settled. They evolve according to the child's age and needs, and the woman's professional circumstances and opportunities—two sets of interests that can be completely contradictory. If the child presents an unexpected problem, the ideal of motherhood, which has thus far been successfully sidestepped, rears up in full force. The mother is inevitably guilty. This specter of the bad mother hovers over a woman all the more oppressively if she has internalized the ideal of the good mother. When confronted by such conflicting demands, both the woman and the mother feel they are falling short. Faced with this scenario, more and more women choose to avoid it.

6

WOMBS ON STRIKE

Today, unlike at the turn of the previous century, there is
no political agenda attached to childbirth;[1] the decision not
to have children (or the lack of a decision leading to the
same result) is a strictly private matter. Most of the time, it
is the outcome of an intimate dialogue between a woman
and herself and has nothing to do with an ideological stance.
What we see is that the phenomenon of childlessness is
steadily becoming more widespread, particularly in English-
speaking countries but also in Japan and throughout southern Europe. In twenty years, the number of childless women
in these places has doubled, almost without anyone noticing.

Referring to this new trend, English-speaking countries
usually distinguish between "childless" and "child-free,"
which implies forgoing the option of having children.

Germans talk of *Kinderlosigkeit*, a word used with similar intent, while in France, where the phenomenon is less prevalent, there is no specific term for this choice. There is no clear distinction between voluntary and involuntary childlessness, or any reference to a particular way of life.

There are an estimated 10 to 11 percent of French women who do not have children and demographers' projections do not anticipate major changes.[2] By contrast, that number reaches 18 percent in England,[3] 20 percent in Italy,[4] 16 percent in Austria (with 25 percent of that figure in Vienna),[5] and between 21 and 26 percent in Germany.[6] The same trend is evident outside Europe. In the United States, where fertility rates remain high, 20 percent of women are childless, which is twice as many as thirty years ago.[7] An Australian study estimated that at least 19.7 percent of Australian women of reproductive age will remain childless,[8] and data from industrialized Asian countries such as Singapore and Thailand point to similar percentages.[9] We do not have figures for childless Japanese women, but we do know that Japan has one of the lowest fertility rates in the world, along with Germany, where it hovers at 1.3 children.[10]

The numbers almost seem to point to some unspoken resistance to motherhood. Evidently, as soon as women are able to control reproduction, pursue studies, enter the job market, and aspire to financial independence, motherhood stops being a natural, self-evident fact, becoming a question instead. Although choosing not to have children is still a decision taken by a minority, the trend constitutes a genuine revolution, suggesting the need to redefine women's identity. Of course, not all industrialized countries are in the same situation. Evolving cultural norms and family policies will influence the choices parents make, but the phenomenon of childlessness, reinforced by the individualism of our age, is not about to disappear, particularly not when it has definite advantages and attractions.

WHERE A MOTHER'S LOT
IS MOST DEMANDING

In those countries most affected by childlessness and declining fertility, there is a combination of two factors that act as powerful deterrents to motherhood. The first and perhaps more important is the prominence of the model of the good mother. The second—which follows from the first—is the lack of family policies that are specifically helpful to women.

THE INFLUENCE OF CULTURAL NORMS

These factors are much in evidence in three large industrialized nations that in other ways are profoundly different from one another: Germany, Italy, and Japan. With strong patriarchal traditions, these countries clung for longer than most to a model in which the sexes were complementary, where a strict distinction existed between men's and women's spheres and roles and tasks were carefully differentiated. Women were in charge of caring for the children, the husband, and the home; men were in charge of everything else.

Historically, this model might have existed almost everywhere, but the three countries in question continue to share an overvaluation of the mother's role to the point where it dominates every other aspect of a woman's identity. The German *Mutter*, the Italian *mamma*, and the Japanese *kenbo*[11] project a mythical aura of motherhood, at once sacrificial and all-powerful. By contrast, the specter of the French *maman* and English *mommy* seems rather insubstantial.

Women who are identified with so exalted a mother figure find themselves prisoners of a role that tethers them to the responsibilities of the home. A mother can hardly escape her burden when it is endorsed by a powerful social consensus. And changing the situation is a formidable challenge when society is ordered by men and for men, who see only advantages in the status quo. Moreover, the moral obligations of the mother's role have been handed down from an earlier generation, one that experienced motherhood as the full scope of a woman's existence.

Nevertheless, since the 1970s, following the example of other industrialized countries, German, Italian, and, more recently, Japanese women gradually entered universities and the job market,[12] striving for freedom, financial independence, and possible reconciliation between their family and professional lives. But often society—even these different societies—has remained deaf to women's expectations. Once they had children, however, these women found themselves staying at home to look after them. Not only is there a desperate lack of child-care facilities in these countries, but should a woman happen to find a solution to the problem of child care, she would have to face the disapproval of her mother and mother-in-law. Entrusting one's child to an institution or a stranger is condemned as maternal desertion.[13] In the workplace, the situation is hardly more inviting: in Japan particularly, discrimination toward mothers of young children is widespread.

The net result is that women put off motherhood till relatively late in life and have fewer children. Although concerned governments have tried to institute supportive family policies, as in Germany,[14] which has invested in better child care for children under three years old, the ideal of the good mother devoted to her children still wields a powerful influence. Changing an ideal takes far longer to have effect than providing child care.

Favoring the Mother at the Expense of the Woman

No country can afford to ignore changes in its birthrate. In the long term, a nation's pension payments, power, and very survival are at stake. To curb the decline in recent decades, some European governments have reevaluated their family policies. In general, however, demographers have identified four approaches, which are largely determined by the structure of a country's traditional social welfare system:

> The Nordic countries have universalistic state policies that promote the independence of individuals and social equality; the state provides most of the welfare (welfare state). English-speaking countries promote market-based individualism; families and the market provide the welfare (liberal welfare states). Central European countries (including France and Germany) have policies geared at preserving the status quo and traditional family forms; they depend mostly on the family to provide welfare (conservative welfare state). Mediterranean countries are like conservative states, but have a stronger family bias (Southern-European welfare state).[15]

A feminist perspective might rearrange those categories into just two groups: countries that implement policies that address the full range of women's ambitions and countries that do not. To put it another way, some welfare policies help women manage their different roles while others serve only to support mothers in their family life. The second type of approach considers all other demands on a woman—those relating to a career—as matters of personal choice, with no connection to government policy. However, the past few decades have shown that assistance helping mothers fulfill their different roles, such as those instituted in Scandinavian countries and to a lesser extent in France, have been most successful.

Those countries with the lowest birthrates—Japan, Italy, Germany—also seem to offer women the least choices. In Japan, as in Italy, birth outside marriage is still greeted with disapproval, as is divorce. Marriages in Japan (which are still frequently arranged) are in decline (the institution is "in the process of collapse,"[16] according to one demographer), and the urge to have children along with it. Reconciling family and working life is considered almost impossible. Most Japanese women stop work when they marry or when their first baby is born. According to a 2006 survey by the Japanese Ministry of Health, a third of women who choose to continue working after marriage leave their jobs in the following four years. Child care is rare and expensive; nursery schools take children from only three years old and close at two in the afternoon. Elementary school begins at age six. In these circumstances, a promise from Japanese prime minister Yukio Hatoyama to award families some $250 a month for each school-age child is unlikely to change the situation. Until very recently, similar conditions—perpetuated by the notion of woman-as-mother, irreplaceable in the care of her child—pertained for German women, particularly in the former Federal Republic of Germany. In the past in both countries, such circumstances left women with very limited options: exclusive motherhood or remaining childless. The varying European experiences show that the best birthrates exist in the countries with the highest rates of working women. However, this is not wholly a function of generous maternity leave and other similar family policies. For women to have more children, they must be able to entrust them to high-quality, full-day child care, and also to have the option of working part-time or flexible hours. In a country like Austria, which devotes 2.3 percent of its GDP to family leave (among the most generous in Europe), there is also a glaring lack of public or private child-care facilities.[17] The result is a low birthrate and a high percentage of childless women, particularly among women with college education.

Germany's example is also instructive. Although Germany has broken free of many of the constraints of the traditional family—marriage with children, remaining single, living together, living apart, being a single parent, or being stepparent are all acceptable choices—the state's family policies have failed to boost the birthrate. These policies provide considerable financial help, but they essentially encourage mothers to remain at home, promoting the role of the father-provider and obliging women to choose between family and work from the moment the first child is born.

Faced with that choice and a rising culture of individualism, German women, particularly those with higher education, began to opt to devote themselves to their work, sparing themselves much emotional turmoil. And increasingly, German women (and men) find themselves preferring the childless life. German men and women both register the lowest desire to have children in Europe. In 2004, a survey of twenty- to thirty-nine-year-olds showed that women in western Germany wanted an average of 1.73 children and those in the east 1.78. The men wanted even fewer: 1.59 in the west and 1.46 in the east.[18]

In an earlier effort to understand Germany's startling decline in the desire to have children, the University of Leipzig conducted a major survey in 1999, canvassing nearly sixteen hundred males and females, parents and non-parents, aged between fourteen and fifty.[19] It came as no surprise that the emotional rewards were the strongest motive for having children, followed by the social approval of parenthood (particularly for Germans in the west). The major obstacles to having children were personal and financial constraints. However, it emerged that children had lost their status as the first priority in people's lives. In fact, when the responders were asked to rank what they most valued, children placed sixth after health, income and financial security, work, relationships and sexuality, and living conditions. Only friends and leisure activities were considered less important. Women wanted children more than men, eastern Germans more than western Germans, and older people more than younger.

The results of this survey do not warrant generalization.

They are not cast in stone and could change depending on various factors. Yet it is possible that they herald a profound change in attitudes and a diversification of women's aspirations that extend well beyond Germany. It is particularly worth noting that it is German women who are turning their backs on anything to do with motherhood: the greatest resistance to the desire to have a child is coming precisely from women in a country where a mother's role is especially burdensome. Of course, for some women having a child in the home involves a way of life that simply does not suit them. It is doubtful whether any kind of family policy, however far-reaching, would help change their minds. And for the rest, generous leave and good child care are a beginning, requiring significant public investment. But that is still not enough. Sharing the job market has to be mirrored by partners sharing family-related tasks,[20] which can only be achieved by profound feminist reform right through society, as much in politics as in industry, and most significantly among men. No country is yet in a position to boast that it has achieved the goal of sexual equality.[21]

THE EMERGENCE OF A NEW WAY OF LIFE

Until recently, only a rare few women thought they could live happily without children. Rarer still were those who admitted that they did not enjoy child rearing and regretted the experience of motherhood. Until recently, becoming a mother signaled a woman's coming of age and without that passage, happiness and achievement were unattainable. Women who slipped through the net of motherhood were regarded with suspicion or condescension, freely referred to as "dried up," "frustrated," "unfulfilled." Popular imagination cast childless women as sad and lonely (unlike the cheerful bachelor) because there could be no life of companionship outside of marriage, and no marriage without children.

These convictions have been smashed by the emergence of people choosing to live without children and women pursuing their professional ambitions. The range of choices that are now acceptable signals the rise of a new hedonism that is crucially important in people's decisions whether or not to become parents.[22] While we might acknowledge that parents are driven by hedonism, too—a ruse on the part of the species to perpetuate itself—we nonetheless tend to more readily dismiss the child-free women as irresponsible and selfish. In fact, the truth is that a woman who chooses not to have children has generally engaged the question of a mother's responsibilities to a degree of seriousness not previously explored, when motherhood was simply a natural necessity.

Internalizing the Ideal Mother

Accounts by childless women and the many surveys of them that are now available are striking for their faithful endorsement of the model of the perfect mother. Even these women believe that a good mother takes constant care of her children round the clock and cannot pursue personal fulfillment at the same time. They cannot conceive of taking on the responsibility of children while also being the teacher, artist, doctor, or executive they want to be. How can you take proper care of a baby while you're writing your thesis? These women have thoroughly internalized the perspective of La Leche League and child psychologists, for whom motherhood and a career are incompatible.

Journalist Émilie Devienne reflects this view in a book that is extremely blunt about choosing not to have a child.[23] Referring to Edwige Antier and state children's advocate Claire Brisset, Devienne chides mothers who are in too much of a hurry to respect the time their child needs, women who put their children into care too early (before the age of two or three) or send them to school too soon, women who cut corners to off-load their tasks as mothers. "You have to be clear-sighted," she says, "and know whether, all day and every day, you want to enlist in this kind of relationship which ideally should be unshakeable and unconditional." She feels that motherhood (or fatherhood) should not be taken on as a "loving impulse, or an experiment, or a philosophy of life. It is first and foremost a duty we have the freedom to impose on ourselves and whose repercussions go far beyond our private lives. Either you take that on or you abstain."

Adopting this all-or-nothing logic while maintaining a high ideal of motherhood, women like Devienne make no reference to the pleasures and benefits of child rearing. They see only the dutiful side, the constraints and sacrifices. In one psychologist's interviews conducted with childless women, some interviewees expressed disgust at the physical aspects of motherhood, not only pregnancy and birth but also caring for a child.[24] Others claimed they found the idea of looking after a baby full-time depressing, "like spending all day in the exclusive company of an incontinent mental defective."[25] Some worried about the monotony of dirty, repetitive, and unrewarding tasks. They feared feelings of alienation and loss of identity. But according to the American sociologist Kristin Park, who has reviewed most of the surveys carried out on child-free men and women in the last twenty years, the primary and most frequently cited reason for their decision (in 79 percent of surveys) is freedom.[26] These people prized their emotional and financial autonomy, their freedom of movement, and their ability to take advantage of every opportunity for personal fulfillment. The second reason, mentioned in 62 percent of surveys, is marital happiness. After that came professional and financial considerations, fear of overpopulation, and lack of interest or a dislike of children.

For a very long time, and perhaps still to this day, such explanations for not wanting children were considered unseemly rationalizations of unresolved subconscious conflict. Childlessness was a negative choice that suggested psychological issues: a poor relationship with the mother,[27] a rejection of womanhood,[28] "questionable narcissistic motivations,"[29] depressive tendencies, or low self-esteem. This was a pathological rejection that only psychoanalytic treatment might be able to sort out.

It is true that a good many women interviewed about their decision not to have children have talked about the frustrations of their own mothers, who were burdened by worry and responsibility and who handed on an unappealing model.[30] At the same time, though, these studies also include active mothers who encouraged the interviewees to pursue their studies and achieve independence[31] without in any way discouraging them from marrying and having children.

Overall, there seems to be little ground for analyzing the choice of motherhood in terms of normal or deviant. We do not ask questions about the legitimacy of the wish to have children, although we are all aware of the devastation caused by irresponsible mothers. How many children are brought into the world to play roles of compensation or distraction? How many children are abused, neglected, or abandoned? This subject remains unexplored. Society seems more concerned with women who try to assess their responsibilities rigorously than with those who take them on with little reflection.

Familial and Professional Satisfaction

In France, most scholars who study the family do not believe that our age of individualism[32] ultimately favors coupledom over parenthood. As Pascale Donati points out, opinion polls confirm that family is still considered the highest value and that "a child is deemed indispensable to marital stability."[33] The majority of French family professionals concur on the benefits that parenthood brings to individuals, strengthening their identities and physical and psychological well-being. While the social and professional costs of motherhood to women are clearly articulated, the cost to marriage does not generally figure prominently in studies.

However, a few English and American researchers have taken up the question of satisfaction among couples both with and without children. Studies of those with children suggest some interesting conclusions, showing as they do flagging happiness as parents reach their forties. It is only relatively recently that the connection has been made between this tendency and the fact that there are frequently young children in the home at this time.[34] It is clear that children impede parents' ability to talk to each other and often make it hard for the couple to find necessary time alone. While bringing up a child is one recognized cause of friction between couples, the difficulty of alternating between being a parent and a partner exacerbates the problem. A relationship founded on love and support depends on a necessary minimum of intimacy and freedom to thrive. But being a parent requires that you forgo yourself and your desires to be available for your children.

And nothing could be more at odds with a mother's (or

father's) role than being a lover. When the children go to bed and the exhausted couple is finally alone together, they may well have some trouble discarding their behavior as parents and shifting into a seductive mood. Thus the idea that a child reinforces a couple's stability cannot be assumed. Of course a child forges an unbreakable link between the mother and the father, but he can also present a real trial for the understanding between the man and the woman.

Childless couples, on the other hand, take pleasure in the advantages of being alone: living for each other, doing more things together than parents are able to do, paying more attention to the other person's feelings and desires. They see children as a possible threat to the harmony they are able to take for granted.[35]

People who choose not to have children also generally settle down with one partner later in life. Their individualism tends to be evident in other characteristics: they have little or no interest in religion; they are tolerant, cosmopolitan, egalitarian, and city-dwelling.[36] With all their advantages, however, childless couples seem to split up just as frequently as those with children, and almost certainly more easily.[37] Thus one set of choices is not necessarily more conducive to success than another, although the legitimacy of childlessness deserves recognition.

Whether they live alone or as part of a couple, childless women, according to all the surveys carried out over the last thirty years, make a significant commitment to their professional lives. Studies confirm that that more childless women work (87 percent against 75 percent) and they more often hold senior managerial positions[38] (36 percent against 21 percent of mothers). In 2000, journalist Elinor Burkett noted that childless women were highly represented among America's elite, being wealthier, more independent, and better educated than the average mother. She also made the point that the numbers of voluntarily childless women are greatest among those who are university educated or highly qualified. The higher the qualification and the more interesting the job, the more likely a woman is to choose to remain childless: "Amongst those without high-school diplomas, only 10 percent have foresworn reproduction, rising to 19 percent amongst the two-year-degree set, reaching an astonishing 28 percent amongst four-year graduates."[39]

Some sociologists see nothing surprising in these findings: in one article on motherhood in the United States, the authors note: "Because more educated women have greater economic opportunities and more alternative sources of self-esteem than less-educated women, the rational choice perspective suggests that level of education will be inversely related to the importance of motherhood."[40] They point out that although black women in the United States have higher birthrates than white, this changes with their level of education. In both cases, gaining high qualifications goes hand in hand with having children later and having fewer of them.

This link between the level of education and childbirth is evident almost everywhere.[41] In a study carried out by the Australian Bureau of Statistics, 20 percent of women with an undergraduate degree or higher remained childless, while only 9 percent of women without these qualifications had no children.[42] German demographer Jürgen Dorbritz points out that the number of childless German women born between 1955 and 1960 fluctuates at around 30 percent, but the percentage is higher among the most qualified women born after 1960: 35.3 percent for those born in 1964 and 38.5 percent for those in 1965.[43] Demographer Isabelle Robert-Bobée finds a similar trend in France. Of those women born between 1945 and 1953, 10 percent had no children, but 16 percent of them were among the most highly qualified, with 7 percent among the least qualified. Among women who finished their studies six years later than their generation's average, 20 percent had no children (12 percent for those who lived with a partner) against 12 percent for those who finished their studies just two years later than the average.

Robert-Bobée echoes others when she says that "the most highly qualified women can hope for social recognition through their work whereas, for the less qualified, this recognition is more likely to come from achieving the status of parenthood." From an economic point of view, she adds, "the price paid in terms of lost opportunities as a result of having a child is higher for women at management level and rises in direct relation to the size of their salaries." It seems that highly qualified women feel sufficiently fulfilled by their professional activities to forgo other hopes and dreams, even if they could easily afford child care.

If this trend were to become widespread, perhaps we might begin to see a phenomenon of motherhood for hire, or motherhood confined to those with greater cultural, social, and professional limitations. Or, as the American demographer Phillip Longman points out, to the most religious, traditional, and conservative women.[44] Looking at the numbers, Longman predicts a return to patriarchy, the only "cultural regime" that can maintain the high birthrate necessary to ensure that nations survive and pensions are paid. He sees early signs of such a tendency in the embrace of religion in the United States and in the practices of observant Muslims. But this conservative prediction overlooks both the growing power of individualism and the profound impact of the feminist revolution.

Maligned yet Envied

There is still a strong tendency to view childlessness in a woman as a failure. A woman without children tends to receive either pity or rebuke. As Pascale Donati said, "Non-procreation is a departure from the norm"[45] that comes with a price of social disapproval. After carrying out a series of interviews with thirty women aged forty to fifty and thirty men aged forty-five to fifty-five, none of whom had children, she concluded:

> If you do not have children but could have done, it is
> better to be a man than a woman, to live alone rather
> than with a partner, and, if you are a woman, not to make
> it too obvious that you feel fulfilled. On this scale, being
> a married woman who has chosen not to be a mother is
> the most suspect. . . . Our society has established an
> acceptable period for self-sufficiency in a loving relation-
> ship, that is, the time it takes to meet and settle down
> together. But people are expected to move beyond this
> period and seek a more altruistic connection—parenthood.
> Surely a woman who refuses to be a mother enjoys love-
> making rather too much?[46]

There are plenty of negative stereotypes about such women:
selfish, incomplete, insecure, immature, materialistic, career-
driven,[47] and more.

Émilie Devienne observed that a non-mother is constantly
expected to justify herself, as if, by contrast, mothers never
display questionable motives or behaviors.[48] A non-mother
is subject to pressure from parents, family, friends (who
are parents), colleagues, in short, from all sides. With such
pressure, it makes sense that having a child can come to feel
like more of a duty than a desire.[49]

There are a number of indications that the state of non-parenthood is in fact secretly envied by some parents, who might admit to such feelings in private conversation[50] or anonymous surveys but will not say so explicitly. The aggressive censure of childlessness is one such sign. For parents who regret having children, how could they acknowledge disappointment with the emotional gain after having made so many sacrifices to attain it? So selfish and calculating a view of parenthood and, worse, motherhood is inadmissible and therefore unsayable. Society is not ready to hear that some parents feel frustrated and bitter and would perhaps have done better without children.

Nonetheless, childless women have been growing more acceptable in the last twenty years. French social scientist Odile Bourguignon has predicted that "women who do not want to have children will probably soon be given permission by our culture not to, reserving motherhood for women who want it."[51]

IN SEARCH OF A NEW DEFINITION
OF WOMANHOOD

Demographers and sociologists anticipate a rise in the phenomenon of childlessness by choice. In France "it is likely that among younger cohorts more women will have no children, but the projected increase in childlessness is limited: 11 percent of women born in 1970 may ultimately remain childless."[52] This modest increase—also projected for Scandinavian women—compares strikingly with anticipated figures for the rest of Europe. British sociologist Rosemary Gillespie, who has studied the trend toward childlessness,[53] estimated in 2003 that 25 percent of English women born in 1973 would not have children.[54] Similar figures have been put forward for former Eastern bloc countries and southern Europe.

But these statistics rely on several unknowns: Could realistic assessments of the costs and benefits of parenthood better equip prospective mothers than the expectations of adventure and emotional reward they currently associate with having children? A more reasonable approach to motherhood, along with a less restrictive model and family policies that support sexual equality, might go a long way to disprove the predictions of childlessness. Even in the absence of such shifts, and despite Phillip Longman's projection, it is hard to imagine a return to patriarchy.

But even if the proportion of childless women were to remain only at today's level, traditional definitions of women as mothers no longer hold. For a significant number of women, having children is no longer the summit of their aspirations. Not only do they reject the equivalence of womanhood with motherhood, they consider themselves more truly female than women whose fulfillment stops with their children. To some, the behavior associated with motherhood strips women of their sexuality.[55] Children are associated with "sacrifice." The urge to have children is alien; the notion of maternal instinct carries no meaning. But it is absurd to exclude such women from womanhood or resort to the pathological diagnoses of the past.

Childless women have been hailed as pioneers in a new phase of feminism by such figures as Rosemary Gillespie and Mardy Ireland of the United States. Ireland points out that "the 1970s gave rise to the concept of androgyny . . . with the androgynous individual exhibiting characteristics of both sex roles. Now, in the 1990s, some intently question whether human characteristics need to be dichotomized and defined by gender at all."[56] According to Catherine Hakim, the answer is that they do not. Child-free women, she says, prove there are no absolute or essential characteristics of women that distinguish them from men.[57]

This idea would horrify both those who fear similarity between the sexes to the point of confusion and the advocates of women as female mammals who call them to fulfill their maternal instincts. But whether we like it or not, motherhood is now only one important aspect of women's identity, no longer the key to achieving a sense of self-fulfillment. Since the advent of contraception, women's identities have splintered and diversified. The inability to acknowledge this smacks of willful blindness.

7

FRENCH WOMEN:
A SPECIAL CASE

French mothers have a bad reputation, which they owe to an old practice that is considered contrary to nature and morality: removing the baby from the mother unusually early. In the 1700s they entrusted their newborns to wet nurses; today they hand them over to child-care facilities or nannies. Judging from statistics, it is clear that French mothers are not all that keen on staying at home or breast-feeding. This attitude, so unlike that of most of their contemporaries, has elicited a good deal of disapproval from psychologists and anthropologists. As early as the 1920s, renowned anthropologist Bronislaw Malinowski referred to French women as "notable aberrations."

At the moment of birth, the mother's instinctive impulses are approved and reinforced by society which, through various customs, moral rules, and ideals, sees the mother as the child's wet nurse and nanny. This is the case in both the upper and lower classes in almost all European nations. And yet, even with such a fundamental, biologically endorsed relationship, there are societies in which certain customs, as well as a weakening of instinctive impulses, give rise to notable aberrations. A case in point is the system whereby a child is removed from the mother for the first year of his life and given to paid nannies. At one point, this custom was very widespread among the French middle class; as was the almost equally regrettable custom of protecting the mother's breasts by hiring a wet-nurse or feeding the child with artificial milk.[1]

According to Pascale Pontoreau, the "concept of a good mother did not exist"[2] in France traditionally. It seems it still does not exist in France. Most mothers balk at the idea of giving up work, even in the first year of their child's life, and most of them bottle-feed. Public events like La Leche League's "Big Nurse-Ins,"[3] held in big cities to encourage breast-feeding, mostly draw smiles, shrugs, and sarcasm.

There is a fairly direct line of descent from the unworthy mother of the eighteenth century to the mediocre mother of today, which is full of implication for the historic social status of French women. That social status, along with a nonchalant approach to motherhood, might perhaps explain the country's high birthrate, a phenomenon that all demographers find surprising. Although French women are also drawn to childlessness, they have the most children. The key to this apparent paradox lies in the past.

MEDIOCRE MOTHERS BUT MOTHERS NONETHELESS

As we have seen, Scandinavian women are Europe's champions of breast-feeding champions while the French are at the bottom of the league. The two nationalities share the highest rate of professional activity in Europe, although French mothers continue to work full-time, particularly after the birth of their first child. With the second and, more noticeably, the third child, the numbers of working mothers decline: nearly 50 percent with one child work full-time compared to 25 percent with three or more children.[4]

While the Scandinavians and Dutch opt to work part-time, most French mothers see that as more of an imposed constraint than an advantage. Only 22 percent of French women aged twenty to forty-nine work part-time: 21 percent of working mothers with one child, 32 percent with two, and 45 percent with three. Overall, few women want to work less: only 9 percent of twenty- to forty-nine-year-olds who don't have access to part-time work wish that they did.[5] Part-time work is often a sign of weak job security and is used by companies more as a means of adjusting the payroll than as relief for busy mothers.

Given the high numbers of working mothers, the French birthrate poses a conundrum. Most recently estimated by the French National Institute for Statistics and Economic Studies (INSEE) at 2.0 children per woman, it was the highest in all twenty-seven European countries for 2008.[6] François Héran, director of the National Institute for Demographic Studies (INED), suggests three explanatory factors for this "French exception." First, free nursery schools that take children at three years old (and sometimes younger—a French invention); second, broad, flexible arrangements for couples (most children are now acceptably born out of marriage);[7] and last, many women who plan pregnancies after the age of forty.[8]

These factors go hand in hand with another notable feature: France is world champion when it comes to contraception.[9] In 1997, out of one hundred women between the ages of fifteen and forty-nine who had partners and claimed they did not want to become pregnant, eighty said they were using a method of contraception. This figure is much higher than the global average (58 percent) and slightly above the average for Europe and North America (72 percent). However, this does not stop French women, unlike their Irish Catholic counterparts, for example, from maintaining a high abortion rate: more than 210,000 a year.

One frequent assumption is that France's high birthrate is due to the country's immigrant population. but according to demographer Laurent Toulemon and others, this supposition "is not valid: The overall level of childbirth in the 1990s would be a mere 0.07 child per woman less if it were based only on women born in France. Furthermore, immigrants' daughters born in France have exactly the same total fertility as women born to mothers themselves born in France."[10]

As a last resort, demographers explain this French phenomenon by pointing to the country's family policies, which are fairly unusual and, according to some, even unclassifiable. They are certainly generous, given that family spending has risen to 3.8 percent of GDP (including tax benefits), and puts France in third position among OECD countries, where the average is 2.4 percent,[11] yet they are not as far-reaching as those in Denmark and Iceland.

French family policies are, however, more diversified than elsewhere, providing significant (if still inadequate) support for mothers who interrupt their careers to look after children under the age of three. After the introduction of paid parental leave in 1985, to help the parents of three children, the Provision of Services for Young Children, introduced in 2004, extended the policy by allowing parents—which generally means mothers—to stop work for six months when they have their first child. But in addition to stopping work, mothers were also helped to go back to their jobs. A "dual benefits system was set up [to provide] parents with access to child care so that they can continue to work, but also to let mothers decide instead to . . . look after a young child."[12] The introduction of alternatives signaled respect for the diversity of parents' choices. There are similar benefits in Finland and Norway.

Nonetheless, French family policies are still not as good as they could be. They lack two important features that could persuade women to have more children. Despite the existence of paternity leave (in 2002 fathers became entitled to two weeks of paid leave after the birth of a child, three in the case of multiples), there is little incentive for fathers to share domestic work and child care with their partners, whereas Scandinavian countries have made moves to encourage men in this direction. Furthermore, women—who are more frequently unemployed than men—are given little help in the job market, and policies concerning flexible hours to accommodate working mothers are tragically inadequate. Last, high-quality child care is still not an automatic given. French mothers certainly enjoy unusual privileges, but their circumstances are far from ideal, yet, as we have seen, the fertility rate remains high. This suggests that family policies alone, even those as far-reaching as in some Scandinavian countries, do not fully account for whether or not women decide to have children.[13]

AN OLD TRADITION:
THE WOMAN BEFORE THE MOTHER

We have to go back several centuries to understand the behavior of contemporary French women. Since the seventeenth century, and especially the eighteenth, the model of the ideal woman has not been limited to motherhood. Quite the opposite, in fact: motherhood was held at a distance. For the ideal woman, being a mother was a duty necessarily performed to pass on a husband's name and inheritance but was insufficient to define her. Indeed, the job of mothering was deemed incompatible with the duties of a distinguished woman and wife.

Aristocratic French women, free of material concerns, were the first to practice the art of child-free living. In fact, the first wet nurse agency opened in Paris as early as the thirteenth century. In the seventeenth century, upper-class women handed their children over to wet nurses from the moment of birth. But in the 1700s, this phenomenon spread to urban society.[14] From the very poorest to the richest, in large and small towns, it became general practice to send children away to wet nurses, often very far from their home. The least fortunate mothers, who were forced to work away from home in order to survive, might not have had any choice. But this was not the case for women in more comfortable circumstances, the same women who sought to conform to the accomplished ideal.

In order of importance, that ideal meant being first a wife, then a figure in society, and finally a mother. Breast-feeding and caring for children were clearly obstacles to the first two priorities. Women (and their families) who considered themselves above the common people considered breast-feeding as ridiculous as it was disgusting.[15]

Husbands and fathers were also responsible for this rejection of breast-feeding and of child care. Children were a hindrance to pleasure. Not only did some men complain that their wives smelled strongly of milk, but doctors at the time forbade sexual activity for the duration of breast-feeding (as well as during pregnancy). Since it was thought that sperm spoiled the milk by curdling it, fathers were forced into a long period of abstinence, during which they might be lured away from the marital bed to commit adultery.

Families, in-laws, doctors, and moralists, believing that family cohesion was threatened by the arrival of a baby, encouraged new mothers to place their children with wet nurses. All of society approved of this practice, and women themselves did not seem to complain about it. Quite the opposite, as we see in a number of contemporary accounts in which the women seem to delight in the fact of sending their children away. As well as being an obstacle to her sex life, a young child got in the way of a woman's social life. When a child came home from the wet nurse, he was immediately entrusted to another paid caregiver, the governess (followed by a private tutor for boys), before being sent away at the age of eight or nine to boarding schools or convents.

In the Age of Enlightenment, it seems, a woman's duties as a mother were negligible. Looking after a child was not considered sufficiently gratifying, nor were day-to-day chores. Women who put their ease and pleasure first respected the view articulated by historian Fustel de Coulanges:

> *Was there ever a less charming bother*
> *Than a gaggle of infants who wail?*
> *One cries father, one cries mother,*
> *The other calls both without fail.*
> *And all that this pleasure will incur*
> *Is being called no better than a cur.*

Women from the privileged classes found their fulfillment in social life: receiving guests and paying visits, showing off new clothes, going for walks, attending the theater. A socialite would be out gambling every night until the early hours. Then she would "enjoy peaceful sleep, or at least only interrupted by pleasure."[16] And "noon found her in bed."[17] She was untroubled by pangs of conscience toward her children because her community agreed that social life was a necessity, a fact confirmed by doctors themselves. Physician Moreau de Saint-Élier, for example, said, in the mid-eighteenth century, that looking after children "was an embarrassing responsibility . . . in society." Off-loading them gradually became a mark of social distinction.

The lower middle class, the wives of tradesmen or local judges, were eager to imitate their more fortunate sisters. For want of a dazzling social life, they might adopt the trappings of an enviable status by consigning their own maternal duties to paid help. It was better to do nothing at all than to appear preoccupied with something so undistinguished.

The result was that at a time when there was no substitute for breast milk and when standards of hygiene were abysmal, babies died like flies. During the Ancien Régime, mortality in children under one year was over 25 percent and nearly one child in two did not reach the age of ten.[18] These statistics were changeable, according to how babies were fed and cared for. As a general rule, half as many children kept and fed by their own mothers died as those sent to wet nurses: between 11 and 19 percent, depending on the location and the conditions.

This fact, which remains shocking to scholars of the family and especially in public opinion, did not derive solely from the fact that children had not yet been granted their present protected status. It was also rooted in women's desire to define a broader role for themselves and emancipate their lives from exclusive motherhood, which brought them no appreciation. Liberated from the burdens common elsewhere, eighteenth-century French women (and English) from the highest ranks of society enjoyed the greatest freedom of any women in the world.[19]

Unlike their peers in Mediterranean Europe, they were at liberty to come and go as they pleased as participating members of society. Indeed, their presence and wit were considered necessary ingredients for refined society. In the cities, they held salons and worked to surround themselves with men and women of consequence. To be successful, it was not enough to dispense the odd well-chosen word: they were required to perfect the subtle art of conversation and keep up-to-date with current affairs. Some achieved a degree of local notoriety and others a level of historic glory. Women who embodied female distinction and left their names inscribed in eighteenth-century history were cultured and knowledgeable and sometimes childless, or they performed the basic maternal duty to have children and arrange for them the best possible marriages.

This unusual model of emancipation is the heritage of modern French women: their identity is not restricted to the role of mother. Despite the more demanding role for mothers that emerged at the end of the eighteenth century[20] and held until the advent of feminism, French society still has a singular approach to the status of women.

French Women Today

The triumph of Rousseauian naturalist philosophy, the rise of the bourgeoisie, the pro-birth ideology of the late nineteenth century, and the later psychoanalytic revolution all radically changed the status of children. A precious, unequaled asset to society and his parents, a child warranted assiduous maternal care. Women were required to be attentive, responsible mothers who breast-fed and kept their children in the home. As historian Edward Shorter put it, women took "the sacrifice test."[21] But it was not done without reticence and resistance in wealthier circles where mothers continued to bring wet nurses from the countryside into their homes—a practice that lasted until Pasteur discovered sterilization and opened the way for the widespread use of bottle-feeding.

The striking thing, however, about French mothers in the nineteenth and twentieth centuries is that, despite an evolving ideology of the good mother devoted to her children, nonchalant and indifferent mothers succeeded in slipping through the net of social opprobrium. A woman had to be genuinely cruel, like the mother in *Carrot Top*,[22] to incur disgrace. Right until the end of the Second World War, in spite of doctors' solemn warnings against the bottle and their promotion of breast-feeding,[23] many mothers turned a deaf ear, and with the father's approval.

Bottle-feeding, which thrived after the war, was considered a compromise aimed at reconciling a woman's personal pursuits with her duties as a mother. Bottle-feeding meant a woman had freedom of movement and could be replaced as her child's caregiver, therefore restoring the ability to be both mother and woman. Now, at the beginning of the twenty-first century, most French women pursue a triple role: wife, mother, and professional. Motherhood represents only one factor in a woman's fulfillment, necessary but not sufficient in itself. Women do not intend to give up any aspect of their lives, neither motherhood, which they come to later and later,[24] nor their other ambitions.

French women thus present a special case because, unlike most Europeans, they have the benefit of historic recognition of their identities beyond motherhood. Just as eighteenth-century society readily accepted sending babies to wet nurses, so twenty-first-century society considers bottle-feeding and child care perfectly legitimate. The existence of child-care facilities and nursery schools for very young children shows that society supports a model of part-time mothering. Grand-mothers, mothers-in-law, and fathers do not complain. It is understood that only the mother can choose how to manage her life in her and her children's best interests. There is no moral or social pressure bearing on a woman to be a full-time mother, not even in the first year after birth. French society acknowledged a long time ago that the mother need not be the only party responsible for her child.

Although they are constantly admonished to take on their fair share of parental and household chores,[25] French fathers continue to contribute very little in this area. But in their place, the state shares responsibility for the baby's well-being and upbringing. And because the state's duty toward the mother and the child is universally accepted, that public opinion tends to be far more scathing about the state's shortcomings than about any failure on the part of the mother or, especially, the father.

Tolerant and blame-free, this collective attitude plays a positive role in women's decision to have children. The lighter the burden on the mother and the greater the respect given to her choices as a woman, the more likely she is to want the whole experience of child raising, and even to repeat it. Supporting part-time motherhood is the key to increased fertility. Conversely, insisting that the mother sacrifice the woman seems to delay her decision to have a child and possibly discourages her from having one at all.

For How Long?

For nearly three decades, a subterranean ideological war has been fought for a wholesale return to nature. We cannot yet assess its consequences for women. The reverence for all things natural glorifies an old concept of the maternal instinct and applauds masochism and sacrifice, constituting a supreme threat to women's emancipation and sexual equality.

The advocates of this philosophy have an extraordinary weapon on their side: a mother's guilt. Naturalism has been with us for thousands of years. History provided dazzling example of the efficiency of such guilt when Rousseau succeeded in convincing women and society to recommit to the exclusive role of the mother through guilt.[26] Women everywhere heard the moralizing heaped on Sophie, the future wife of Émile in Rousseau's eponymous book, loudly and clearly, particularly those who had nothing to give up. Respect for mothers: there at last was an improvement in women's status.

Women are no longer in the same position. They play a significant role in society, and if they all began to stay at home for two or three years after the birth of each child, the economy would feel the effect. But the fact that we can even entertain the notion of a wholesale return to the home shows that playing on women's guilt eventually works on their minds. If women are subjected to the relentless message that a mother must give her child everything—milk, time, energy—or pay for it later, inevitably more and more of them will give in.

The greatest enemy of naturalism is individualism and its hedonistic promise. Although some women are fulfilled by the rewards of naturalism, everyone else sooner or later works out the advantages and disadvantages of all-embracing motherhood. It is an incomparable experience of giving life and receiving love; it is also a daily diet of frustration and stress, self-sacrifice and conflict, along with feelings of failure and guilt. Contrary to the claims of naturalism, love is

not a given, not a mother's for a child, nor the child's for its
parents, who might find themselves enfeebled and alone in
old age, with no recompense for their sacrifice.

Hedonistic individualism wants the pleasures without
the pains, or at least prefers the pleasures. If almost one-third
of German women choose childlessness, it must be because
they feel that becoming mothers is not worth the cost. If 38.5
percent of the most highly qualified women decide against
having children, it must mean that they are fulfilling their
potential through something other than the kind of motherhood imposed on them. The proponents of ideal motherhood
as they see it had better heed the message before it is too late.

For now, French women have avoided the dilemma of
all-or-nothing motherhood. They have successfully resisted
the decrees of pediatricians. But can they hold out against
the naturalists, who have such solid support from institutions around the world? Can they stand firm against the
doctors and nurses in charge in the maternity ward? Against
the escalating rhetoric of guilt? Although financial crisis
and economic instability are hardly conducive to social resistance, it seems that young women in France are still doing
exactly as they please.

But for how long?

NOTES

FOREWORD

1. Elisabeth Badinter, *Mother Love: Myth and Reality—Motherhood in Modern History* (New York: Macmillan, 1981).

PART ONE: THE STATE OF PLAY

1. THE AMBIVALENCE OF MOTHERHOOD

1. "Vouloir un enfant" (Wanting a child), *Psychologies*, http://www.psychologies.com/Famille/Maternite/Desir-d-Enfant/Articles-et-Dossiers/Vouloir-un-enfant.

2. Survey participants were allowed to give more than one answer.

3. A question loosely inspired by Marian Faux's book *Childless by Choice: Choosing Childlessness in the Eighties* (Garden City, NY: Anchor Press/Doubleday, 1984), p. 28.

4. Marie Darrieussecq's *Le bébé* (Paris: POL, 2002); Nathalie Azoulai's *Mère agitée* (Paris: Seuil, 2002); Éliette Abécassis's *Un heureux événement* (Paris: Albin Michel, 2005); and Pascale Kramer's *L'implacable brutalité du réveil* (Paris: Mercure de France, 2009).

5. Abécassis, *Un heureux événement*, p. 15.

6. Kramer, *L'implacable brutalité du réveil*, p. 17.

7. Darrieussecq, *Le bébé*, p. 98.

8. Ann Landers, "70 Percent Say: No kids," *Chicago Sun-Times*, January 23, 1976. See Faux, *Childless by Choice*, p. 2.

9. The experiment was tried again several times in the 1980s by the founder of the Childfree Network, Leslie Lafayette. During radio shows, she asked listeners—who were promised anonymity—to answer the same question. The negative replies varied from 45 to 60 percent. Again, the only significance of these figures is that they give voice to people who are disappointed by the reality of parenthood. The figures give no indication of what percentage this group genuinely represents.

10. An expression borrowed from Jean-Claude Kaufmann, *L'invention de soi* (Paris: Armand Colin, 2004), p. 276.

11. *Domestic Injustice*, or *Injustice ménagère*, is the title of a collection published in 2007, edited by the sociologist François de Singly.

12. See Beth Anne Shelton and Daphne John's 1993 survey published by François de Singly in the 2004 afterword of *Fortune et infortune de la femme mariée* (Paris: Presses Universitaires de France, 1987), p. 218. See also the very recent article by Arnaud Régnier-Loilier, "Does the Birth of a Child Change the Division of Household Tasks Between Partners?" *Population and Societies*, no. 461 (November 2009). He stated that "the arrival of a child

widens the gender imbalance in the sharing of household tasks, generally at the expense of women," which contributes to alienating her from the job market. Today, as in the past, women take on the bulk of household chores, which become incrementally more demanding with successive births. The author emphasized the fact that "women's dissatisfaction [with the sharing of household tasks] increases after the birth of a child."

13. Singly, *Fortune et infortune de la femme mariée*, p. 215.

14. Ibid., p. 221: Table on the division of work according to gender and qualifications, National Institute of Statistics and Economic Studies, Time Use Survey, 1998–1999.

15. Ibid., p. 222.

16. The sources for this table and the one below were Eurostat, various national institutes of statistics, and the United Nations. The tables were compiled by the National Institute for Demographic Studies and can be viewed at http://www.ined.fr/fr/pop_chiffres/pays_developpes/indicateurs_fecondite/.

17. Decrees governing the enforcement of relevant laws were published sporadically between 1969 and 1972.

18. Interestingly, demographer France Prioux points out that the birthrate in mixed-race couples has risen, although the rate of this rise has slowed since 2007. See "L'évolution démographique récente en France: l'espérance de vie progresse toujours," *Population-F* 63, no. 3 (2008): 437–76.

19. By "partnership" I mean marriage, common-law marriage, and cohabitation.

20. Laurent Toulemon, "Très peu de couples restent volontairement sans enfant," *Population*, nos. 4–5 (July–October 1995): 1079–110.

21. See Jean-Paul Sardon, "Evolution démographique récente des pays développés," *Population-F* 57, no. 1 (January–March 2002): 123–70; and Isabelle Robert-Bobée, "Ne pas avoir eu d'enfant: plus fréquent pour les femmes les plus diplômées et les hommes les moins diplômés," *France, portrait social*, National Institute of Statistics and Economic Studies, 2006, p. 182.

22. Australian Bureau of Statistics, "Women in Australia, 2007," Australian Government, 2007.

23. As the term *maternal instinct* is not always well received, I have chosen this alternative.

24. It is worth noting that the last two categories, women who do not want children and those who want them at any cost, are often both regarded with a degree of contempt.

25. Catherine Hakim, *Work-Lifestyle Choices in the 21st Century* (Oxford, UK: Oxford University Press, 2000), p. 6.

26. Ibid., p. 8.

27. Ibid., p. 9.

28. Ibid., p. 10.

29. Neil Gilbert, *Mother's Work: How Feminism, the Market, and Policy Shape Family Life* (New Haven, CT: Yale University Press, 2008), pp. 31–32.

30. In the sense given by Max Weber. These categories are not exhaustive and leave out a number of exceptions, cases that fall outside their margins.

31. Gilbert, *A Mother's Work*, pp. 31–32.

32. Ibid., pp. 32–33.

33. Ibid., pp. 33–34. It is worth noting that these women have little help in the home and that domestic services are expensive.

PART TWO: THE ASSAULT OF NATURALISM

1. "The philosophical belief that everything arises from natural properties and causes" (*Oxford English Dictionary*, 6th ed. [Oxford, UK: Oxford University Press, 2006]), p. 632.

2. Complete U-turns in pediatrics in the last hundred years are well documented in Geneviève Delaisi de Parseval and Suzanne Lallemand's book *L'art d'accommoder les bébés* (Paris: Seuil, 1980).

3. This is how pediatrician T. Berry Brazelton introduces himself in *Touchpoints: Birth to Three* (Cambridge, MA: Da Capo Press, 2006).

2. THE SACRED ALLIANCE OF REACTIONARIES

1. In its literal sense, as those who respond to an action with an opposite reaction that tends to cancel it out. For this definition, I've relied on linguist Alain Rey's *Dictionnaire historique de la langue française* (Paris: Le Robert, 2006).

2. Ibid.

3. Michel Serres, *Le contrat naturel* (Paris: François Bourin, 1990).

4. See Gérard Vienne's film *The Monkey Folk*, 1989.

5. *L'Événement du jeudi*, June 8–14, 1989.

6. See Isabelle Curtet-Poulner, "Ces femmes anti-pilules," *Le Nouvel Observateur*, January 3, 2008.

7. Ibid., quoting a 2007 survey by the National Institute for Prevention and Health Education-BVA.

8. Éliette Abécassis and Caroline Bongrand, *Le corset invisible* (Paris: Albin Michel, 2007), p. 187; *IARC Monographs on the*

Evaluation of Carcinogenic Risks to Humans, vol. 91, *Combined Estrogen-Progestogen Contraceptives and Combined Estrogen-Progestogen Menopausal Therapy* (Lyon, France: International Agency for Research on Cancer, 2007), p. 91; D. Cibula, A. Gompel, A. O. Mueck, C. La Vecchia, P. C. Hannaford, S. O. Skouby, M. Zikan, L. Dusek, "Hormonal Contraception and Risk of Cancer," *Human Reproduction Update* 16, no. 6 (2010): 631–50.

9. Besides the incidence of alcohol in cancer of the pharynx, the oral cavity, the esophagus, and the liver, in March 2007 the IARC announced that it might also be responsible for colorectal and breast cancer.

10. Marc Mennessier, "Alcool: l'abstinence totale n'est pas préconisée," *Le Figaro*, July 28, 2009. The HCSP restated its recommended alcohol consumption for adults: not to exceed two glasses of wine a day for women and three for men. It concluded: "There is not at present any conclusive argument to justify modifying our current recommendations . . . in favor of total abstinence."

11. "Environnement chimique et reproduction" colloquium (November 25, 2008), in *Madame Figaro*, December 16, 2008. According to Professor Pierre Jouannet, the danger is presented by "certain phthalates, molecules found in cosmetics, food packaging and plastics," as suggested by studies on rats. *Elle* magazine sounded the same alarm in its December 1, 2008, issue.

12. An ancient Greek word meaning "female slave." A doula helps a woman during pregnancy, childbirth, and the first stages of motherhood.

13. *Femme actuelle*, February 2008. All for a remuneration of around $750 in 2007.

14. Study published by Marshall H. Klaus, John H. Kennell,

and Phyllis H. Klaus, *The Doula Book: How a Trained Labor Companion Can Help You Have a Shorter, Easier, and Healthier Birth* (New York: Perseus Books, 2002), chap. 5. Another study (2003), cited by *Femme actuelle*, February 2008, claims that having a doula present during labor "aids spontaneous birth and reduces the need for pain relief."

15. *Le Figaro*, October 8, 2008. The article points out that, according to the French home birth organization AAD (Accouchement à domicile), 25 percent of women would like to give birth at home but are prevented by the shortage of midwives available (there are only about sixty in France).

16. Report of the Maternity Services Review, Australian Department of Health and Ageing, 2006.

17. On a pain scale of 1 to 10, the pain of childbirth is considered by most people to be 10.

18. Elsbeth Kneuper, "Die Natürliche Geburt. Eine globale Errungenschaft?" in A. Wolf and V. Hörbst, eds., *Medizin und Globalisierung: Universelle Ansprüche—lokale Antworten* (Berlin: LIT Verlag, 2003), pp. 107–28.

19. *Marie Claire*, February 1987. Having seen this anonymous account, an obstetrician consulted by the magazine pointed out that an injection of the morphine-based drug Dorosal bears no comparison to an epidural because it alters consciousness and inhibits the mother's proper involvement.

20. Pascale Pontoreau, *Des enfants, en avoir ou pas* (Montreal: Les Éditions de l'Homme, 2003), p. 53.

21. Ibid.

22. Frédérick Leboyer, *Pour une naissance sans violence* (Paris: Seuil, 1974).

23. Yvonne Knibiehler, *La révolution maternelle: femmes, matér-nité, citoyenneté depuis 1945* (Paris: Perrin, 1999), p. 194.

24. Nevertheless, when a recent self-consciously aesthetic film called *Le premier cri* (2007) aimed to show the beauty of child-birth across the world, from Masai tribes to Ho Chi Minh, from Mexico to Siberia and to the Nigerian desert (where the viewer is subjected to the unbearable pain of a Tuareg mother giving birth to a stillborn baby), an *Elle* magazine journalist (October 29, 2007) was one of very few to react. Incensed by the militant out-pourings of a Quebec woman who wanted to give birth naturally in her alternative, eco-friendly community, refusing all medical assistance even if her life was in danger, the journalist reminded readers that somewhere in the world a woman dies every minute giving birth, and that even in developing countries more than ten thousand newborns die every day as a result of complications in childbirth.

25. See next chapter.

26. Although the European Food Safety Authority confirmed that, given the minimal admissible levels of BPA, baby bottles presented no risk, the City of Paris has banned them from munic-ipal day-care centers.

27. "Le bien-être de bébé version écolo," *Le Monde*, Novem-ber 7, 2007; and *Le Figaro*, April 21, 2008.

28. Interview with Nathalie Kosciusko-Morizet on Europe 1 and i-Télé, September 14 and 15, 2008. Besides proposing this tax, she said she found it "wonderful" scrubbing cloth diapers.

29. "Le bien-être de bébé version écolo."

30. Letter of July 7, 1981, addressed to Macmillan Publish-ing, who published *L'Amour en plus: histoire de l'amour maternel*

(XVIIe–XXe siècle) (Paris: Flammarion, 1980) as *Mother Love: Myth and Reality—Motherhood in Modern History* (New York: Macmillan, 1981). This letter did nothing to diminish my admiration for Bruno Bettelheim's extensive work with autistic children, even though I still believe in the virtue of truth. It was partially published by Nina Sutton in 1996 in her biography *Bettelheim: A Life and Legacy* (New York: Basic Books, 1996), pp. 425–26.

31. Diane E. Eyer, *Mother-Infant Bonding: A Scientific Fiction* (New Haven, CT: Yale University Press, 1992), p. 2.

32. Quoted in D. E. Eyer, M. Klaus, P. Jerauld, N. Kreger, W. McAlpine, M. Steffa, and J. Kennell, "Maternal Attachment: Importance of the First Postpartum Days," *New England Journal of Medicine* 286, no. 9 (March 1972): 460–63.

33. Marshall H. Klaus and John H. Kennell, *Maternal-Infant Bonding: The Impact of Early Separation or Loss on Family Development* (St. Louis, MO: C. V. Mosby, 1976).

34. Eyer, *Mother-Infant Bonding*, p. 3. Eyer also notes that social workers responsible for minimizing child abuse warmly welcomed this theory.

35. Marshall H. Klans and John H. Kennell, *Parent-Infant Bonding*, 2nd ed. (St. Louis, MO: C. V. Mosby, 1982).

36. Ibid.

37. In an interview with Bill Moyers on *The World of Ideas*, cited by Eyer, *Mother-Infant Bonding*, pp. 35–36.

38. A few years later T. Berry Brazelton diluted his point. See *Touchpoints: Birth to Three* (Cambridge, MA: Da Capo Press, 2006): "Certain childbirth educators, however, took the implications of the bonding research too literally. . . . Attachment is a long-term process, not a single, magical moment" (p. 37). Similarly, he now

concedes that a young mother can return to work four months after giving birth: "parents need the baby more than she may appear to need them" (p. 80).

39. Jacques Dayan, Gwenaëlle Andro, and Michel Dugnat, *Psychopathologie de la périnalité* (Paris: Masson, Issy les Moulineaux, 2003), p. 13.

40. Various articles by Michael Lamb in the *Journal of Pediatrics* are quoted by Eyer, *Mother-Infant Bonding*, pp. 35–36.

41. "Baby Friendly Hospital" was a label of quality suggested, in 1992, by WHO and UNICEF for hospitals that promoted breast-feeding.

42. Edwige Antier, *Éloge des mères* (Paris: Robert Laffont, 2001), pp. 68–69. My italics. The pointed subtitle of the book is: "Trusting in Maternal Instincts to Ensure That Our Children Flourish."

43. Ibid., pp. 54–55.

44. Margaret Mead, "Instinct and the Origins of Love," *Redbook* 136, no. 2 (December 1970): 39–40.

45. Sarah Blaffer Hrdy, *Mother Nature: A History of Mothers, Infant, and Natural Selection* (New York: Pantheon Books, 1999). The study, "Delayed Onset of Maternal Affection After Childbirth," by K. M. Robson and R. Kumpar, was published in the *British Journal of Psychiatry* 136 (1980): 347–53.

46. But not of the theory of bonding, which she compares to a "Velcro-style attachment" and to the modern version of the ethological process of imprinting. She challenges the way studies on nanny goats and ewes have been extrapolated to women.

47. My italics. Sarah B. Hrdy frequently uses this expression.

48. Hrdy, *Mother Nature*, pp. 536–38.

49. Éliette Abécassis, *Un heureux événement* (Paris: Albin Michel, 2005), pp. 71, 79.

50. "Small" when compared to the tiger unleashed by Betty Friedan, whose book *The Feminine Mystique* (1963) sold millions of copies worldwide.

51. Alice Rossi, "A Biosocial Perspective on Parenting," *Daedalus* 106, no. 2 (Spring 1977): 1–31.

52. Her article was fiercely criticized the following year in a book by Nancy Chodorow, which caused a considerable stir: *The Reproduction of Mothering: Psychoanalysis and the Sociology of Gender* (Berkeley: University of California Press, 1978), pp. 18–20.

53. Maryse Guerlais, "Vers une nouvelle idéologie du droit statutaire: le temps de la différence de Luce Irigaray," *Nouvelles questions féministes*, nos. 16–18 (1991): 65.

54. Cited by Hrdy, *Mother Nature*, p. 3.

55. Carol Gilligan, *In a Different Voice* (Cambridge, MA: Harvard University Press, 1982), p. 29.

56. Sigmund Freud, "Femininity," in *Freud on Women: A Reader*, ed. Elisabeth Young-Bruehl (New York: W. W. Norton, 1990), pp. 361–62. Freud attributed this moral deficit to penis envy in the female psyche.

57. Antoinette Fouque, *Il y a deux sexes* (Paris: Gallimard, 1995), p. 157.

58. Feminists as indisputable as Erica Jong and Betty Friedan were eventually won over by maternalism, the former in an interview given to *Vanity Fair* in April 1986, the latter in the second edition of *The Second Stage*, reissued in 1998.

59. Colette Guillaumin, *Sexe, race et pratique du pouvoir: l'idée de nature* (Paris: Côté-femmes, 1992). Nicole-Claude Mathieu,

L'anatomie politique: catégorisations et idéologies du sexe (Paris: Coté-femmes, 1991). Marie-Claude Hurtig, Michèle Kail, and Hélène Rouch, eds., *Sexe et genre: de la hiérarchie entre les sexes* (Paris: CNRS, 1991). Christine Delphy, *L'ennemi principal 1. Économie politique du patriarcat* and *L'Ennemi principal 2. Penser le genre* (Paris: Syllepse, 1998 and 2001). The review *Questions féministes* (1977–1980) followed by *Nouvelles questions féministes* (since 1981).

3. MOTHERS, YOU OWE THEM EVERYTHING!

1. See T. Berry Brazelton, *Touchpoints: Birth to Three* (Cambridge, MA: Da Capo Press, 2006).

2. Yvonne Knibiehler, *La révolution maternelle: femmes, maternité, citoyenneté depuis 1945* (Paris: Perrin, 1999), pp. 209–91.

3. Lille, October 2004.

4. Claude Dreux and Gilles Crépin, "Prévention des risques pour l'enfant à naître," *Bulletin de l'Académie nationale de médecine* 190, no. 3 (2006): 713–23.

5. *Le Figaro*, December 26, 2008.

6. Jonathan Winickoff et al., "Beliefs About the Health Effects of Thirdhand Smoke and Home Smoking Bans," *Paediatrics* 123, no. 1 (2009): 74–79.

7. Ibid.

8. Press release of September 11, 2006, under the aegis of the Ministry of Health.

9. A U.S. study published in 2003 found that 15.1 percent of American women continued to drink alcohol during pregnancy (Heather A. Flynn et al., "Rates and Correlates of Alcohol Use

Among Pregnant Women in Obstetrics Clinics," *Alcoholism: Clinical and Experimental Research* 27, no. 1 [January 2003]: 81–87), while 21.7 percent smoked while pregnant (Renee D. Goodwin et al., "Mental Disorders and Nicotine Dependence Among Pregnant Women in the United States," *Obstetrics & Gynecology* 109, no. 4 [April 2007]: 875).

10. Éliette Abécassis, *Un heureux événement* (Paris: Albin Michel, 2005), p. 28.

11. The name was chosen by Mary White's husband—an obstetrician and advocate of natural childbirth—inspired by a statue of the Madonna in Saint Augustine, Florida, honoring "Nuestra Senora de la Leche y Buen Parto"—Our Lady of Easy Delivery and Plentiful Milk.

12. See Lynn Y. Weiner, "Reconstructing Motherhood: The La Leche League in Postwar America," *Journal of American History* 80, no. 4 (March 1994): 1357–81; Christina G. Bobel, "Bounded Liberation: A Focused Study of La Leche League International," *Gender & Society* 15, no. 1 (February 2001): 130–51; Gilza Sandre-Pereira, "La Leche League: des femmes pour l'allaitement maternel (1956–2004)," *Maternités, CLIO*, no. 21 (2005): 174–87.

13. Linda M. Blum, *At the Breast: Ideologies of Breastfeeding and Motherhood in the Contemporary United States* (Boston: Beacon Press, 1999), p. 4. The sociologist pronouncing these two principles states that they characterize contemporary motherhood.

14. Glenda Wall, "Moral Constructions of Motherhood in Breastfeeding Discourse," *Gender & Society* 15, no. 4 (August 2001): 592–610.

15. See http://www.llli.org/philosophy.html?m=1,0,1.

16. Weiner, "Reconstructing Motherhood," p. 1370.

17. Vicky Debonnet-Gobin, *Allaitement maternel et médecine générale* (thesis for doctorate of medicine, Université de Picardie Jules Verne/Faculté de médecine d'Amiens, September 26, 2005), p. 9.

18. *Allaitement maternel: les bénéfices pour la santé de l'enfant et de sa mère*, 2005, published by the French Ministry of Solidarity, Health and Family.

19. Jean Rey, "Breastfeeding and Cognitive Development," supplement, *Acta Paediatrica* 92, no. 5442 (August 2003): S11–S18; Geoff Der et al., "Effect of Breast Feeding on Intelligence in Children," *British Medical Journal* 333, no. 7575 (October 4, 2006): 945, http://www.bmj.com.

20. Pierre Bitoun, "Valeur économique de l'allaitement maternel," *Les dossiers de l'obstétrique* 216 (April 1994): 10–13. Dr. Bitoun is a pediatrician and a member of the EU Promotion of Breastfeeding project. Several calculations of this kind have been done in other countries. See T. M. Ball and A. L. Wright, "Health Care Costs of Formula-feeding in the First Year of Life," *Paediatrics* 103 (1999): 870–76.

21. A figure put forward by Debonnet-Gobin in her thesis, *Allaitement maternel et médecine générale*, p. 10.

22. Ibid., p. 11.

23. See http://www.llli.org/philosophy.html?m=1,0,1.

24. See http://www.alternamoms.com/nursing.

25. Even though pediatricians recognize that formula is increasingly well-adapted to a baby's nutritional needs. Debonnet-Gobin, *Allaitement maternel et médecine générale*, p. 28.

26. Reported by Claude Didierjean-Jouveau, former president

of the French LLL and current editor in chief of the review *Allaiter aujourd'hui*, in Sandre-Pereira, "La Leche League," p. 5.

27. Edwige Antier, *Éloge des mères* (Paris: Robert Laffont, 2001), p. 166.

28. Edwige Antier, *Confidences de parents* (Paris: Robert Laffont, 2002), p. 113.

29. Edwige Antier, *Vive l'éducation!* (Paris: Robert Laffont, 2003), p. 13.

30. Elisabeth Badinter, *Mother Love: Myth and Reality—Motherhood in Modern History* (New York: Macmillan, 1981), pp. 186–90. See also Marilyn Yalom, *A History of the Breast* (New York: Alfred A. Knopf, 1997).

31. *Allaiter aujourd'hui*, 1993, p. 3 n. 16.

32. Weiner, "Reconstructing Motherhood," p. 1368.

33. Robin Slaw, "1999 LLLI Conference Sessions: Promoting Breastfeeding or Promoting Guilt?" *New Beginnings* 16, no. 5 (September–October 1999): 171.

34. Weiner, "Reconstructing Motherhood," p. 1375.

35. Viviane Antony-Nebout reports that in 1989 UNICEF estimated that five thousand children under the age of five died every day of diarrhea and respiratory infections because they were not breast-fed; in other words, 1.5 million every year in developing countries. See Viviane Antony-Nebout, *Hôpital Ami des bébés: impact sur l'allaitement, militantisme ou respect des femmes?* (doctoral thesis, Université de Poitiers, 2007), p. 20.

36. Ibid., pp. 24–25.

37. Ibid., p. 23.

38. It stipulates that a child has the right to enjoy the best possible state of health, specifically breast-feeding.

39. Every facility providing maternity services and care for newborns must meet the following requirements: (1) Have a written breast-feeding policy that is routinely communicated to all health care staff. (2) Train all health care staff in the skills necessary to implement this policy. (3) Inform all pregnant women about the benefits and practice of breast-feeding. (4) Help mothers initiate breast-feeding within half an hour of birth. (5) Show mothers how to breast-feed and how to maintain lactation even if they should be separated from their infants. (6) Give newborn infants no food or drink other than breast milk, unless medically indicated. (7) Practice rooming-in—that is, allow mothers and infants to remain together—twenty-four hours a day. (8) Encourage breast-feeding on demand. (9) Give no artificial teats or pacifiers to breast-feeding infants. (10) Foster the establishment of breast-feeding support groups and refer mothers to them on discharge from the hospital or clinic.

40. In June 1991, during a meeting of the International Association of Pediatricians.

41. One just has to read the introductory text of the Innocenti Declaration to be convinced that LLL has won on every point: "Breastfeeding is a unique process that:

- provides ideal nutrition for infants and contributes to their healthy growth and development;

- reduces incidence and severity of infectious diseases, thereby lowering infant morbidity and mortality;

- contributes to women's health by reducing the risk of breast and ovarian cancer, and by increasing the spacing between pregnancies;

- provides social and economic benefits to the family and the nation;

- provides most women with a sense of satisfaction when successfully carried out . . .

- these benefits increase with increased exclusiveness of breastfeeding during the first six months of life, and thereafter with increased duration of breastfeeding with complementary foods."

42. "Breastfeeding Report Card—United States, 2010," Center for Disease Control, http://www.cdc.gov/breastfeeding/pdf/2011BreastfeedingReportcard.pdf.

43. See http://www.40.statcan.gc.ca/101/cst01/health92b=eng.htm.

44. Australian Bureau of Statistics, "Breastfeeding in Australia," Australian Government, 2001.

45. 2002 statistics. Extract from the IPA (L'association Information Pour l'Allaitement), EU Project on Promotion of Breastfeeding in Europe, "Protection, Promotion and Support of Breastfeeding in Europe: Current Situation," European Commission, Directorate General for Health and Consumers, Public Health, Luxembourg, December 2003.

46. See http://www.info-allaitement.org/europe-du-nord.html.

47. See http://assoc.ipa.free.fr/CHIFFRES/nord.htm.

48. See http://www.euphix.org/object_document/05130n27421.html.

49. Study by the Austrian Ministry of Health, Family and Youth, published on September 13, 2007, "Kdolsky: neue Studie zum Thema Stillen und dem Ernährungsverhalten von Saüglingen."

It states that 93.2 percent of mothers breast-feed after birth. After three months, 60 percent breast-feed exclusively and 12 percent partially. At six months, these figures are 10 percent and 55 percent, respectively. When the child is one year old, 16 percent are still partially breast-feeding.

50. See http://www.lalecheleague.org/cbi/bfstats03.html.

51. Béatrice Blondel and Morgane Kermarrec, "Les Naissances en 2010 et leur évolution depuis 2003," Institut National de la Santé et de la Recherche Médicale, Paris, 2010.

52. Maternity leaves here are the most generous in Europe: in Norway, they are six months on full salary and twelve months on 80 percent salary.

53. Blondel and Kermarrec, "Les Naissances en 2010 et leur évolution depuis 2003."

54. In 2004, it was estimated that they had 238 group leaders throughout France.

55. *Allaiter aujourd'hui* and *Dossiers de l'allaitement*.

56. LaNutrition: http://www.lanutrition.fr/. *Le Parisien* of March 2, 2009, published the following figures: 65 percent of French women breast-fed on leaving the maternity unit, but two-thirds gave up after one month. Six weeks after giving birth, only 15 percent were still breast-feeding their babies.

57. Internet, Paperblog.

58. Decree of July 30, 1998.

59. Co-ordination française pour l'allaitement maternel (French committee for breastfeeding mothers).

60. Antony-Nebout, *Hôpital Ami des bébés*, p. 45.

61. By late 2011, that figure had increased to twelve.

62. Table published by Antony-Nebout, *Hôpital Ami des bébés,* p. 45.

63. Baby-Friendly Health Initiative Australian website: www .bfhi.org.au.

64. It published a report on the subject in February 2009, apparently voted in unanimously. One academy member even appeared on the France 2 evening news solemnly revealing the endless benefits of breast-feeding.

65. Debonnet-Gobin, *Allaitement maternel et médecine générale,* p. 15. It is worth adding that in the United States, white women breast-feed more than black women.

66. It is, for example, striking to find a page (p. 9) in Debonnet-Gobin's thesis devoted to the benefits of breast-feeding for the newborn (a title in bold letters), which gives equal typographical weight to proven facts, suggested ones, and those "under discussion," as if all three categories were one and the same and could be added together.

67. Debonnet-Gobin, *Allaitement maternel et médecine générale,* p. 65. She adds: "Exclusive breastfeeding continued for six months . . . favors a reduction in the risk of allergies in at-risk babies (father, mother, brother or sister has allergies) . . . , and contributes to preventing obesity later in childhood and in adolescence."

68. Geoff Der is a statistician at the Medical Research Council's Social and Public Health Sciences unit in Glasgow. See the results of this study on the Internet, BMJ: www.bmj.com, October 2006.

69. Ibid.

70. The Medical Academy's report (March 2009), although fairly cautious, continues to promote the role of breast-feeding in a child's intellectual development (p. 4) and settles for citing a 2001 study of 208 newborns, and, with no further commentary, adds: "G. Der casts doubts on the effects of mother's milk on intellectual development" (p. 5). It should be noted that in his 2007 study of Belorussian mothers and infants, Mark Kramer affirmed that breast-feeding is more beneficial than bottle-feeding for cognitive development. Who to believe?

71. Blum, *At the Breast*, pp. 45–50.

72. Elisabeth W. Tavárez, "La Leche League International: Class, Guilt, and Modern Motherhood," *Proceedings of the New York State Communication Association* (2007): 3.

73. Expression borrowed from Marie Darrieussecq, *Le bébé* (Paris: POL, 2002), p. 23.

74. Wall, "Moral Constructions of Motherhood in Breast-feeding Discourse," pp. 603–4.

75. See in particular Lyliane Nemet-Pier, *Mon enfant me dévore* (Paris: Albin Michel, 2003), which challenges the myth of family harmony, and Marie-Dominique Amy, who works with autistic children. In *Construire et soigner la relation mère-enfant* (Paris: Dunod, 2008), pp. 36–37, she writes: "I completely condemn a lack of respect for a mother's choices regarding feeding. In maternity wards, mothers can be told the advantages and disadvantages of breast- and bottle-feeding. But to insist that women who do not want to should breast-feed is absurd. It could contribute to a very distorted early relationship and be very stressful for the mother. Shame on us for contributing to the burden of guilt . . ."

4. THE BABY'S DOMINION

1. From the end of the 1970s right up to the latest edition in 2008, *J'élève mon enfant* lays out both feeding choices with their respective advantages. Even though we can deduce the author has a preference for breast-feeding, bottle-feeding is in no way stigmatized.

2. *The Womanly Art of Breastfeeding*, 2nd ed. (Franklin Park, IL: La Leche League International, 1963).

3. Some of these fathers said they felt swindled if and when they divorced and their wives would not even hear of giving them custody of the child(ren), or of joint custody when it was introduced in 2002.

4. Marie Thirion, *L'allaitement: de la naissance au sevrage* (Paris: Albin Michel, 1994). Edwige Antier, *Attendre mon enfant aujourd'hui* (Paris: Robert Laffont, 2007).

5. Edwige Antier, *Éloge des mères* (Paris: Robert Laffont, 2001), p. 119, my italics.

6. Edwige Antier, *Vive l'éducation!* (Paris: Robert Laffont, 2003), pp. 44–45.

7. Edwige Antier, *Confidences de parents* (Paris: Robert Laffont, 2002), p. 55.

8. Ibid., pp. 52 and 60.

9. Denmark and Norway are equally generous. In Denmark, parental leave is for one year, and some fathers can take up to ten and a half weeks of paid leave. Norway offers almost three years of parental leave to couples, forty-four weeks of which are reimbursed at 100 percent salary.

10. Anita Haataja, "Fathers' Use of Paternity and Parental Leave

in Nordic Countries," Kelafpa, Online working papers 2 (2009): 8, 16.

11. Claude-Suzanne Didierjean-Jouveau, *Partager le sommeil de son enfant* (Saint-Julien-en-Genevois, France: Éditions Jouvence, 2005), p. 49.

12. Ibid., preface by Edwige Antier, pp. 8 and 9.

13. Ibid., pp. 46–47.

14. Ibid., pp. 47–48.

15. *Elle*, August, 13, 2009, interviews with Marcel Rufo and Claude Halmos on co-sleeping.

16. Antier, *Confidences de parents*, pp. 51, 52–53.

17. Éliette Abécassis, *Un heureux événement* (Paris: Albin Michel, 2005), pp. 78–79.

18. Ibid., pp. 79–80.

19. According to a study by psychologists at the University of Denver (USA) covering 218 households, an overwhelming majority of young parents noticed a deterioration in their relationship with their partner after the birth of their first baby.

20. *Moi d'abord* (Me First), the title of Katherine Pancol's book (Paris: Seuil, 1979).

21. Elisabeth Badinter, *Mother Love: Myth and Reality— Motherhood in Modern History* (New York: Macmillan, 1981), pp. 335–60. See also Les Chimères, *Maternité esclave*, vols. 10–18 (Paris: Union General d'Edition, 1975).

22. Lyliane Nemet-Pier, *Mon enfant me dévore* (Paris: Albin Michel, 2003).

23. The APE remunerated (at half the minimum wage) the parent who stopped work in order to look after a child up to the age of three. In 98 percent of cases the parent was the mother.

24. Liza Belkin, "The Opt-Out Revolution," *New York Times Magazine*, October 26, 2003. See also "Quand superwoman rentre à la maison," *Elle*, October 20, 2008.

25. In total, 22 percent of mothers with university degrees; 33 percent of those with MBAs worked part-time; and 26 percent approaching top management did not want to be promoted. The article also indicated that 57 percent of mothers who graduated from Stanford in 1981 stayed at home for at least a year.

26. They can reduce their work time by two hours per day (their salary is then paid pro rata).

27. Many breast-fed children do not go into child care before they are one year old.

28. *Courrier cadres*, no. 28 (March 2009). In "Emploi des mères et garde des jeunes enfants en Europe," *OFCE Review* (July 2004), Hélène Périvier points out that Swedish women do continue to work (albeit with long maternity leaves), but they reduce their average working hours (in their working life) by seventeen hours a week.

29. Catherine Hakim, *Key Issues in Women's Work: Female Diversity and the Polarisation of Women's Employment* (London: Glass House Press, 2004).

30. Mckinsey & Company, *Women Matter 2010*, http://www .Mckinsey.com/locations/swiss/news_publications/pdf/women_ matter_2010_4.pdf.

31. Eurostat, http://epp.eurostat.ec.europa.eu/statistics_ex plained/index.php/gender_pay_gap_statistics.

32. Australian Department of Families, Housing, Community Services and Indigenous Affairs website: www.fahcsia.gov.au.

PART THREE: OVERLOADING THE BOAT

1. Michelle Stanworth, ed., *Reproductive Technologies: Gender, Motherhood, and Medicine* (Cambridge: Polity Press, 1987), p. 14. Carolyn M. Morell also points out that women's situations have become even worse. With the changes that have happened in the work environment and family structure, women's responsibilities in terms of child care are defined far more rigorously than in the past. A mother's responsibilities just keep on increasing. See *Unwomanly Conduct: The Challenges of Intentional Childlessness* (New York: Routledge, 1994), p. 65.

2. See the novels and essays by Marie Darrieussecq, Nathalie Azoulai, Éliette Abécassis, and Pascale Kramer.

3. As Lyliane Nemet-Pier observes with such acuity, a child has become a precious creature but one that must not get in the way. See *Mon enfant me dévore* (Paris: Albin Michel, 2003), p. 12.

5. THE DIVERSITY OF WOMEN'S ASPIRATIONS

1. Pascale Donati, "Ne pas avoir d'enfant: construction sociale des choix et des constraints à travers les trajectories d'hommes et de femmes," *Dossier d'études*, no. 11, Allocations familiales (2000): 22.

2. Pascale Pontoreau, *Des enfants, en avoir ou pas* (Montreal: Les Éditions de l'Homme, 2003), pp. 8–9.

3. Linda M. Blum, *At the Breast: Ideologies of Breastfeeding and Motherhood in the Contemporary United States* (Boston: Beacon Press, 1999), p. 6.

4. Sharon Hays, *The Cultural Contradictions of Motherhood* (New Haven, CT: Yale University Press, 1996), pp. 6–9.

5. A woman who has never had children. The French word *nullipare* is the title of a novel by Jane Sautière (Paris: Verticales, 2008).

6. Sautière, *Nullipare*, p. 13 [translator's note: some liberties have been taken with this extract because the resonance of the French words cannot be reproduced in English].

7. Catherine Hakim, *Work-Lifestyle Choice in the 21st Century* (Oxford, UK: Oxford University Press, 2000), pp. 51–52.

8. Isabelle Robert-Bobée, "Ne pas avoir eu d'enfant: plus frequent pour les femmes les plus diplômées et les hommes les moins diplômés," *France, portrait social*, National Institute of Statistics and Economic Studies, 2006, p. 184: "More than 20% of women born in 1900 had no children as compared to 18% of women born in 1925 and 10 to 11% for the generations born between 1935 and 1960."

9. Pascale Donati, "La non-procréation: un écart à la norme," *Informations sociales*, no. 107 (2003): 45. This group represents 2 to 3 percent of women.

10. Michel Onfray, *Théorie du corps amoureux* (Paris: LGF, Le Livre de Poche, 2007), p. 218.

11. Ibid., pp. 219–20.

12. Rosemary Gillespie, "Childfree and Feminine: Understanding the Gender Identity of Voluntarily Childless Women," *Gender & Society* 17, no. 1 (February 2003): 122–36.

13. Annily Campbell, *Childfree and Sterilized: Women's Decisions and Medical Responses* (London: Cassell, 1999).

14. See the works of the sociologists Jean E. Veevers (Canada) and Elaine Campbell (Great Britain) and the psychologist Mardy S. Ireland (United States), who questioned hundreds of childless

women. In France this question has aroused interest only much more recently: see the works of Pascale Donati, Isabelle Robert-Bobée, and Magali Mazuy.

15. Magali Mazuy, *Être prêt-e, être prêts ensemble? Entrée en parentalité des hommes et des femmes en France* (doctoral thesis in demography, Université Paris I Panthéon-Sorbonne, September 2006).

16. Donati, "Ne pas avoir d'enfant," p. 37.

17. Mardy S. Ireland's term from *Reconceiving Women: Separating Motherhood from Female Identity* (New York: Guilford Press, 1993).

18. Jean E. Veevers, "Factors in the Incidence of Childlessness in Canada: An Analysis of Census Data," *Social Biology* 19, no. 3 (1972): 266–74. See also Veevers, *Childless by Choice* (Toronto: Butterworths, 1980).

19. Leslie Lafayette, *Why Don't You Have Kids? Living a Full Life Without Parenthood* (New York: Kensington Books, 1995). Elinor Burkett, *The Baby Boon: How Family-friendly America Cheats the Childless* (New York: Free Press, 2000). Maryanne Dever and Lisa Saugères, "I Forgot to Have Children!: Untangling Links Between Feminism, Careers and Voluntary Childlessness," *Journal of the Association for Research on Mothering* 6, no. 2 (2004): 116–26.

20. Donati, "Ne pas avoir d'enfant," p. 20.

21. Ibid.

22. JaneMaree Maher and Lise Saugeres, "To Be or Not to Be a Mother?: Women Negotiating Cultural Representations of Mothering," *Journal of Sociology* 43, no. 1 (2007): 5–21. Firsthand accounts and results of semi-structured interviews with a hundred women. This study adds to Leslie Cannold's study, *What, No Baby?:*

Why Women Are Losing the Freedom to Mother, and How They Can Get It Back (Fremantle, Australia: Fremantle Arts Centre Press, 2005).

23. Hays, *The Cultural Contradictions of Motherhood.*

24. Maher and Saugeres, "To Be or Not to Be a Mother?" p. 5.

6. WOMBS ON STRIKE

1. See Francis Ronsin, *La grève des ventres: propagande néo-malthusienne et baisse de la natalité français, XIXᵉ–XXᵉ siècles* (Paris: Aubier Montaigne, 1980).

2. Laurent Toulemon, Ariane Pailhé, and Clémentine Rossier, "France: High and Stable Fertility," *Demographic Research* 19, article 16 (July 1, 2008): 503–56. According to their projections, 11 percent of women born in 1970 and 12 percent of those born in 1980 would remain childless (pp. 516 and 518).

3. Dylan Kneale and Heather Joshi, "Postponement and Childlessness: Evidence from Two British Cohorts," *Demographic Research* 19, article 58 (November 28, 2008): 1935–68. They indicate that 9 percent of women born in 1946 remained childless whereas 18 percent of those born in 1958 and 1970 did.

4. Alessandra De Rose, Filomena Racioppi, and Anna Laura Zanatta, "Italy: Delayed Adaptation of Social Institutions to Changes in Family Behaviour," *Demographic Research* 19, article 19 (July 1, 2008): 665–704. The authors indicate that 10 percent of women born in 1945 remained childless and 20 percent of those born in 1965 (p. 671).

5. Alexia Prskawetz, Tomáš Sobotka, Isabella Buber, Henriette Engelhardt, and Richard Gisser, "Austria: Persistent Low Fertility

Since the Mid-1980s," *Demographic Research* 19, article 12 (July 1, 2008): 293–360.

6. Jürgen Dorbritz, "Germany: Family Diversity with Low Actual and Desired Fertility," *Demographic Research* 19, article 17 (July 1, 2008): 557–98. The author points out that these are estimates: 7 percent of women born in 1935, 21 percent of those born in 1960, and 26 percent of those born in 1966. He also notes that only Switzerland compares with Germany on this subject. *Le Monde*, October 20, 2009, made the point that 29 percent of West German women born in 1965 have remained childless.

7. Figures from 2006 published by the US Census Bureau in August 2008.

8. Australian Bureau of Statistics report, "Women in Australia, 2007," Australian Government, 2007. See also Janet Wheeler, "Decision-making Styles of Women Who Choose Not to Have Children" (paper presented at the 9th Australian Institute of Family Studies Conference, Melbourne, Australia, February 9–11, 2005). See also Jan Cameron, *Without Issue: New Zealanders Who Choose Not to Have Children* (Canterbury, New Zealand: Canterbury University Press, 1997).

9. In Thailand the number of childless women more than doubled between 1970 and 2000, going from 6.5 percent to 13.6 percent. See P. Vatanasomboon, V. Thongthai, P. Prasartkul, P. Isarabhakdi, and P. Guest, "Childlessness in Thailand: An Increasing Trend Between 1970 and 2000," *Journal of Public Health and Development* 3, no. 3 (September–December 2005): 61–71.

10. Like most former Eastern bloc European countries including Russia, but also Greece, Portugal, and Spain. See INED, Indi-

cateurs de fécondité, 2008, Eurostat estimates, http://www.ined.fr/fr/pop_chiffres/pays_developpes/indicateurs_fecondite/.

11. Joanna Nursey-Bray, *"Good Wives and Wise Mothers":* *Women and Corporate Culture in Japan* (thesis submitted to the Centre for Asian Studies at the University of Adelaide, 1992). See also Muriel Jolivet, *Un pays en mal d'enfants: crise de la maternité au Japon* (Paris: La Découverte, 1993). This book describes Japanese women's revolt against the crushing role of the traditional mother.

12. From 1982 to 2007, there was a steady rise in the percentage of Japanese women aged fifteen to thirty-nine who worked. It went from 49.4 percent to 59.4 percent, the rise becoming much more pronounced since 2002. See the Japanese Bureau of Statistics, which can be viewed at http://www.stat.go.jp/english/info/news/1889.htm.

13. In 2004, 62 percent of west Germans (compared to 29 percent in eastern Germany alone) felt that children suffered if the mother worked and that pursuing a career and being a mother were incompatible. Women who tried to do it were perceived as bad mothers, as *Rabenmütter* (mother crows who no longer care for their young when they fall from the nest). Cited by Heike Wirth, *Kinderlosigkeit von hoch qualifizierten Frauen und Männern im Paarkontext: eine Folge von Bildungshomogamie?* (Wiesbaden, Ger.: Verlag für Sozialwissenschaften, 2007), pp. 167–99.

14. Since January 2004, new legislation came into effect with a view to improve child-care facilities for children under three.

15. Toulemon et al., "France: High and Stable Fertility," pp. 505–6.

16. Chikako Ogura, a psychologist and a professor at Waseda University in Tokyo, was quoted by *L'Express*, September 12,

2009, in the excellent report: "Les Japonaises ont le *baby blues*." In Italy, by contrast, women still want to have children—two, on average. Alessandra De Rose et al., "Italy: Delayed Adaptation of Social Institutions to Changes in Family Behaviour," pp. 682–83. The authors pointed out that 98 percent of women aged twenty to twenty-nine would like to have children, that the number of children wanted is an average of 2.1, and that this number remains unchanged even among women who have invested heavily in academic qualifications and have professional ambitions.

17. Prskawetz et al., "Austria: Persistent Low Fertility Since the Mid-1980s," pp. 336–37: in 2005, only 4.6 percent of children under three and 60.5 percent of all children between three and school age benefited from public child care. Furthermore, their opening hours and long closures for holidays made them impractical.

18. Dorbritz, "Germany: Family Diversity with Low Actual and Desired Fertility," pp. 583–84, featuring figures for the number of children people in Germany wanted in 2004 (average).

Number of children	West Germany		East Germany	
	Women	Men	Women	Men
No children	16.6	27.2	5.8	21.1
One child	14.5	13.0	28.7	24.2
Two children	53.7	40.0	50.6	45.0
Three children	11.6	16.2	11.6	7.6
Four children	3.7	3.5	3.3	2.0
Average	1.73	1.59	1.78	1.46

19. Yve Ströbel-Richter, Manfred E. Beutel, Carolyn Finck, and Elmar Brähler, "The 'Wish to Have a Child,' Childlessness and Infertility in Germany," *Human Reproduction* 20, no. 10 (2005): 2850–57.

20. See Ursula Henz, "Gender Roles and Values of Children: Childless Couples in East and West Germany," *Demographic Research* 19, article 39 (August 22, 2008): 1452.

21. The salary gap between men and women is still the best indicator of the situation. We can confirm that it is still universally in men's favor.

22. See the TNS-Sofres survey for *Philosophie Magazine*, "Pourquoi fait-on des enfants? Le sondage qui fait réagir," 27 (March 2009): 21. When asked: "Why have children?" 73 percent of the answers were connected to pleasure.

23. Émilie Devienne, *Être femme sans être mère: le choix de ne pas avoir d'enfant* (Paris: Robert Laffont, 2007), pp. 96–98.

24. Elaine Campbell, *The Childless Marriage: An Exploratory Study of Couples Who Do Not Want Children* (London: Tavistock Publications, 1985), p. 51.

25. Ibid., p. 49.

26. Kristin Park, "Choosing Childlessness: Weber's Typology of Action and Motives of the Voluntary Childless," *Sociological Inquiry* 75, no. 3 (August 2005): 372–402.

27. See Édith Vallée, *Pas d'enfant, dit-elle . . . les refus de la maternité* (Paris: Imago, 2005). Caroline Eliacheff and Nathalie Heinich, *Mères-filles, une relation à trois* (Paris: Albin Michel, 2002).

28. Nicole Stryckman, "Désir d'enfant," *Le Bulletin Freudien*, no. 21 (December 1993).

29. Gérard Poussin, *La fonction parentale* (Paris: Dunod, 2004), quoted in the excellent article by Geneviève Serre, Valérie Plard, Raphaël Riand, and Marie Rose Moro, "Refus d'enfant: une autre voie du désir?" *Neuropsychiatrie de l'enfance et de l'adolescence* 56, no. 1 (February 2008): 9–14.

30. See Jane Bartlett, *Will You Be Mother? Women Who Choose to Say No* (New York: New York University Press, 1994), pp. 107–11; Elaine Campbell, *The Childless Marriage*, pp. 37–41; Marian Faux, *Childless by Choice: Choosing Childlessness in the Eighties* (Garden City, NY: Anchor Press/Doubleday, 1984), pp. 16–17.

31. Pascale Donati, "Ne pas avoir d'enfant: construction sociale des choix et des constraints à travers les trajectories d'hommes et de femmes," *Dossier d'études*, no. 11, Allocations famiales (2000): 15.

32. Philippe Ariès, "L'enfant: la fin d'un règne," in "Finie, la famille?" *Autrément série* "Mutations" (1992): 229–35. Philippe Ariès attributes the decline in birthrates to hedonistic Malthusianism. We have shifted from the child-king to the child-hindrance who compromises fulfillment for the individual and the couple.

33. Donati, "Ne pas avoir d'enfant," pp. 31–32.

34. Faux, *Childless by Choice*, pp. 42–43; Cameron, *Without Issue*, pp. 61–64 and 74–76.

35. Marsha D. Somers, "A Comparison of Voluntarily Child-free Adults and Parents," *Journal of Marriage and the Family* 55, no. 3 (August 1993): 643–50. Cameron, *Without Issue*, p. 75. Sherryl Jeffries and Candace Konnert, "Regret and Psychological Well-Being Among Voluntarily and Involuntarily Childless Women and Mothers," *International Journal of Aging and Human Development* 54, no. 2 (2002): 89–106.

36. Sandra Toll Goodbody, "The Psychosocial Implications

of Voluntary Childlessness," *Social Casework* 58, no. 7 (1977): 426–34. See also Joshua M. Gold and J. Suzanne Wilson, "Legitimizing the Child-free Family: The Role of the Family Counselor," *Family Journal* 10, no. 1 (January 2002): 70–74.

37. Park, "Choosing Childlessness," p. 375. She points out that surveys on comparative marital satisfaction in couples with or without children produced different conclusions. According to some, there is no significant difference; others found there was greater satisfaction within childless couples. In 1995 the British Office of Population Census and Survey showed that the divorce rate is higher in parents of children under the age of sixteen and lower in those with children over this age. The divorce rate for childless couples lay in between the two.

38. Cameron, *Without Issue*, p. 23.

39. Elinor Burkett, *The Baby Boon: How Family-friendly America Cheats the Childless* (New York: Free Press, 2000), p. 182.

40. Julia Mcquillan, Arthur L. Greil, Karina M. Shreffler, and Veronica Tichenor, "The Importance of Motherhood Among Women in the Contemporary United States," *Gender & Society* 22, no. 4 (August 2008): 480.

41. The Swedish demographers Jan M. Hoem, Gerda Neyer, and Gunnar Andersson published a very interesting article exploring the subtleties of this statement. According to them, it is less the level of education that is the determining factor than the professional orientation chosen. When women choose a feminized job (public service, teaching, medical world, etc.), they have more children than those committed to masculine territories (private enterprise, jobs with irregular working hours). However, they bring to light some counterexamples to their hypothesis that limit the

scope of their ideas. See "Education and Childlessness: The Relationship Between Educational Field, Educational Level, and Childlessness Among Swedish Women Born in 1955–59," *Demographic Research* 14, article 15 (May 9, 2006): 331–80.

42. Australian Bureau of Statistics, "Births, Australia, 1998," http://www.abs.gov.au/ausstats/abs@.nsf/0/1DECC52B47FC8E2 6CA2569DE002139C1?Open.

43. Dorbritz, "Germany: Family Diversity with Low Actual and Desired Fertility," pp. 570–71. He refers to figures from the 1999–2003 German micro-censuses.

44. Phillip Longman, "The Return of Patriarchy," *Foreign Policy*, February 17, 2006.

45. Pascale Donati, "La non-procréation: un écart à la norme," *Informations sociales*, no. 107 (2003): 44–51.

46. Ibid., pp. 49–50.

47. Gold and Wilson, "Legitimizing the Child-free Family," p. 71.

48. Devienne, *Être femme sans être mère*, pp. 32–38.

49. Ibid., p. 56.

50. See Mardy S. Ireland, *Reconceiving Women: Separating Motherhood from Female Identity* (New York: Guilford Press, 1993), p. 157, and Bartlett, *Will You Be Mother?*, p. 115. The latter comments: "Child-free women often say [that] mothers are jealous of [them]. 'A lot of my friends say that if they had their time over again they would make the same decision as me. They love their children dearly but just feel restricted by them.' "

51. Odile Bourguignon, "La question de l'enfant," *L'Année sociologique* 37 (1987): 93–118. Quoted by Donati, "Ne pas avoir d'enfant," p. 14.

52. Toulemon et al., "France: High and Stable Fertility," p. 516.

53. See Rosemary Gillespie, "Voluntary Childlessness in the United Kingdom," *Reproductive Health Matters* 7, no. 13 (May 1999): 43–53; Gillespie, "When No Means No: Disbelief, Disregard and Deviance as Discourses of Voluntary Childlessness," *Women's Studies International Forum* 23, no. 2 (March–April 2000): 223–34; Gillespie, "Contextualizing Voluntary Childlessness Within a Postmodern Model of Reproduction: Implications for Health and Social Needs," *Critical Social Policy* 21, no. 2 (May 2001): 139–59; and Gillespie, "Childfree and Feminine: Understanding the Gender Identity of Voluntarily Childless Women," *Gender & Society* 17, no. 1 (February 2003): 122–36.

54. Rosemary Gillespie cites predictions in the 2000 *Social Trends* in her article "Childfree and Feminine."

55. Gillespie, "Contextualizing Voluntary Childlessness Within a Postmodern Model of Reproduction," pp. 49–50.

56. Ireland, *Reconceiving Women*, p. 6.

57. Catherine Hakim, *Work-Lifestyle Choices in the 21st Century* (Oxford, UK: Oxford University Press, 2000), p. 82. See also Judith Butler's work on queer theory.

7. FRENCH WOMEN: A SPECIAL CASE

1. Bronislaw Malinowski, *La sexualité et sa répression dans les sociétés primitives* (Paris: Payot, 1932), pp. 19–20. This text is quoted by the psychoanalyst Hélène Deutsch and spoken as her own words in *La psychologie des femmes*, vol. 2, *Maternité* (Paris: Presses Universitaires de France, 2002), pp. 2–3.

2. Pascale Pontoreau, *Des enfants, en avoir ou pas* (Montreal: Les Éditions de l'Homme, 2003), p. 30.

3. To encourage women to breast-feed on demand and wherever they are, followers of the La Leche League have been organizing public breast-feeding days in all major French cities since 2006. In 2006, five hundred mothers took part; in 2009, twenty-two hundred of them did, according to *Le Parisien* of October 12, and twenty-four hundred, according to the organizers.

4. Olivier Thévenon, "Les politiques familiales des pays développés: des modèles contrastés," *Population et Sociétés*, no. 448 (September 2008).

5. Laurent Toulemon, Ariane Pailhé, and Clémentine Rossier, "France: High and Stable Fertility," *Demographic Research* 19, article 16 (July 1, 2008): 533.

6. INSEE predictions published in August 2009. Only Icelandic women, with 2.1 children per woman, do better. But this nation is not yet integrated in Europe. The synthesized figure for births per woman in Ireland is 2.0, as it is for Norwegians, when the European average is 1.5. See Gilles Pison, "Tous les pays du monde," *Population et Sociétés*, no. 458 (July–August 2009).

7. *Le Figaro*, August 24, 2009. In 1994, 275,248 children were born out of wedlock compared to 465,526 in wedlock. In 2008, they formed the majority: 435,156 compared to 393,248.

8. Ibid.

9. Magali Mazuy, *Être prêt-e, être prêts ensemble? Entrée en parentalité des hommes et des femmes en France* (doctoral thesis in demography, Université Paris I Panthéon-Sorbonne, September 2006), pp. 153–54. The statistics cited are taken from an article by

Henri Leridon and Laurent Toulemon, "La régulation des naissances se généralise," *Cahiers de l'INED*, no. 149 (2002): 477–95.

10. Toulemon et al., "France: High and Stable Fertility," p. 522.

11. Thévenon, "Les politiques familiales des pays développés."

12. Ibid.

13. The opposite case is proved by the United States, where family policy is much less generous than in most European countries and yet the birthrate is significantly higher.

14. Elisabeth Badinter, *Mother Love: Myth and Reality—Motherhood in Modern History* (New York: Macmillan, 1981), pp. 52–136. In 1780, the lieutenant general of the Paris police force, Lenoir, estimated that of the twenty-one thousand children born annually, fewer than one thousand were breast-fed by their mothers, one thousand were breast-fed by a wet nurse at home, and all the rest were sent to wet nurses in the country. Prost de Royer established similar figures in Lyon.

15. Ibid., p. 85. The word *ridiculous* frequently appears in correspondence and memoirs from the period. Mothers, mothers-in-law, and midwives advised young mothers not to breast-feed because it was not seemly for a lady to expose her breasts the whole time to feed her baby. Besides the fact that it gave a bestial image of women as "dairy cows," the gesture itself was immodest. A breast-feeding mother therefore had to be hidden from the world, interrupting her social life for a considerable time.

16. François-Vincent Toussaint, *Les Moeurs*, 1748.

17. Madame Leprince de Beaumont, *Avis aux parents et aux maîtres sur l'éducation des enfants*, 1750.

18. François Lebrun, "25 ans d'études démographiques sur la France d'Ancien Régime: bilans et perspectives," *Historiens et géographes*, October 1976.

19. See Abbé de Pure's *La Précieuse*, 1656–58: "The sweetest thing about our France is that of women's freedom; and it is so great across the entire kingdom that husbands there are almost without power and women reign supreme."

20. Badinter, *Mother Love*, part 2, "A New Honor: Mother Love."

21. Edward Shorter, *The Making of the Modern Family* (New York: Basic Books, 1976), p. 264.

22. Jules Renard, *Carrot Top*, first published by Flammarion in Paris in 1894 and widely known in France.

23. Geneviève Delaisi de Parseval and Suzanne Lallemand, *L'art d'accommoder les bébés* (Paris: Seuil, 1980), pp. 101–5.

24. The average age for having a first child is close to thirty. *Le Monde*, October 20, 2009.

25. Jane Bartlett from the UK feels that sharing these chores is a key factor in reproduction. See *Will You Be Mother? Women Who Choose to Say No* (New York: New York University Press, 1994). According to the latest surveys, fathers have made no progress in twenty years. Mothers still take on four-fifths of household chores. See Arnaud Régnier-Loilier, "L'arrivée d'un enfant modifie-t-elle la répartition des tâches domestiques au sein du couple?" *Population et Sociétés*, no. 461 (November 2009).

26. Badinter, *Mother Love*, pp. 195–231.

ABOUT THE AUTHOR

ELISABETH BADINTER is the acclaimed author of three seminal works on feminism—*Mother Love: Myth and Reality*—*Motherhood in Modern History, Dead End Feminism*, and *XY: On Masculine Identity*—which have been translated into fifteen languages. For many years, Badinter taught philosophy at the École Polytechnique in Paris, where she lives.